Patrols 1942–44

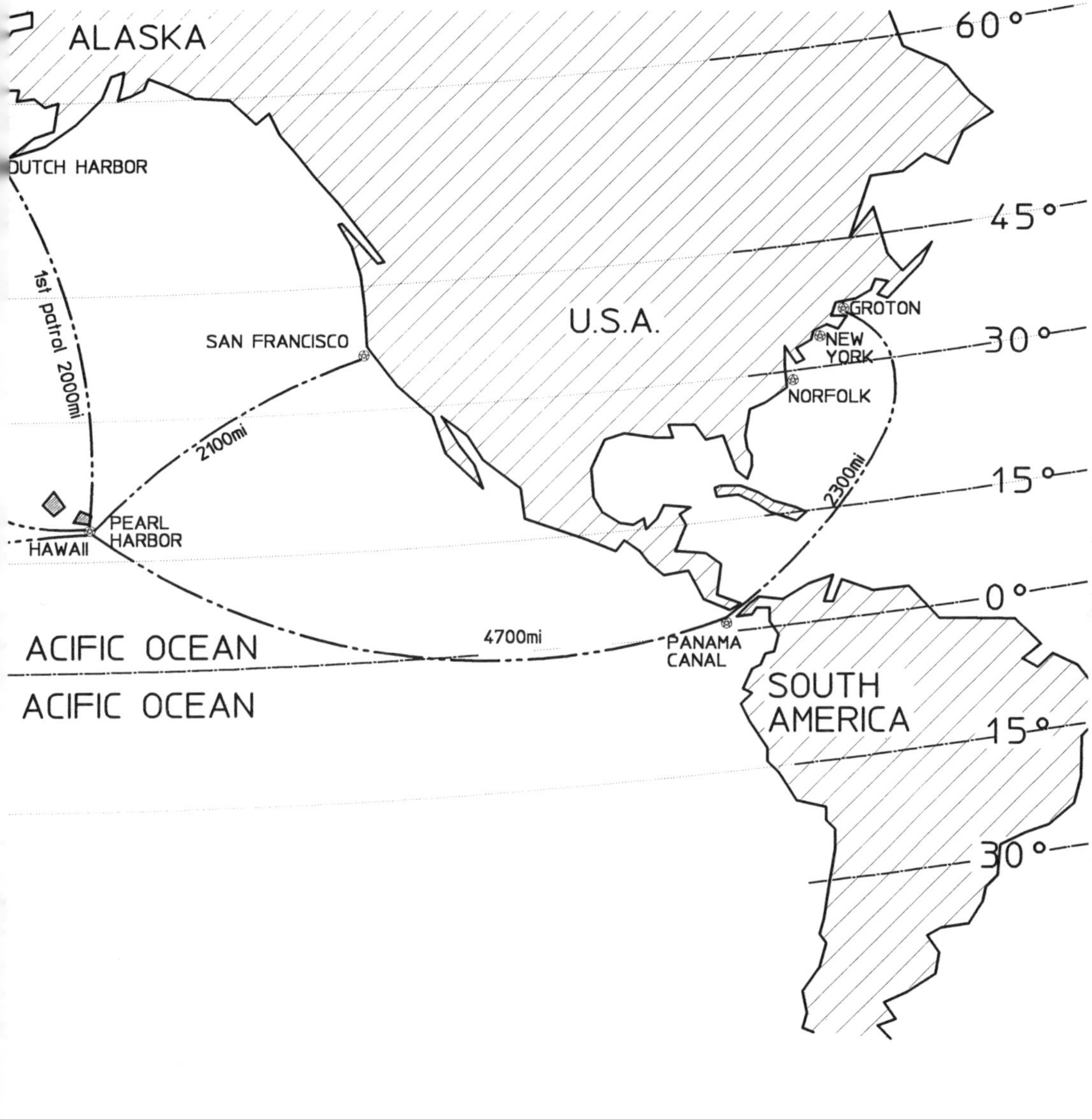

Kangaroo Express

The epic story of the submarine *Growler*

With recollections by "Skipper" Arnold Schade

Kangaroo Express
The epic story of the submarine *Growler*

With recollections by "Skipper" Arnold Schade

Richard J. Lanigan

R J L Express Publications

Book design and production by Tabby House
Manufactured in the United States of America
Library of Congress Catalog Card Number: 97-69729
ISBN: 0-9659995-0-5
Cover design: Foster & Foster
Photo credits:
U.S. Navy
William F. "Radar" Hagendorn
Robert A. "Bob" Link
Leonard Greenwood
Charles Trumbull
Arnold F. Schade

Cover photo: Declassified U. S. Navy photograph of *Growler* in Brisbane, Australia, alongside the tender *Fulton*, February 1943, showing damage to the bow received while ramming and sinking the Japanese ship *Hayasaki*. The men on the tug are, l. to r.: Delbert Hilsabeck, an unidentified sailor from a different boat, and W. R. "Little Stinky" Davis.

The author appreciates the cooperation and generosity the Lockwood family for their permission to include material previously published in *Down to the Sea in Subs* written by their father, Adm. Charles A. Lockwood.

R J L Express Publications
1604 Mission Valley Boulevard
P. O. Box 175
Laurel. FL 34272

Acknowledgments

Kangaroo Express is an epic of the United States Submarine Force during World War II, the USS *Growler*, and of her second skipper, Arnold F. Schade and crew. Their valiant actions played a major part in defeating a powerful imperial aggressor. Today, the world is safer because of the power American Submarine Force.

I wish to acknowledge the many *Growler* veterans who have provided me with personal information and advice upon which I have relied with gratitude:

Vice Admiral Arnold Frederic Schade, USN (ret.), William R. Davis, Leonard D. Greenwood, William F. Hagendorn, editor, *Kangaroo Express Newsletter*, Robert A. Link, Edward A. Packwood, Comdr. Charles P. Trumbull, USN (ret.) and Louis R. McFall.

Other contributors are: Cass Kuhl, son of *Growler* veteran, (the late) Lewis Kuhl; National Archives; Capt. William J. Ruhe, USN (ret.); U.S. Department of the Navy, Rebecca Schade and Jim and Linda Salisbury.

I also want to acknowledge Roy W. Johnson who has been my mentor for many years and has been a tremendous help to me in publishing this book.

Richard J. Lanigan

Contents

Foreword

Salmon follow a predestined course. After "birth" they head down river to the open sea, remaining there until the clock of life beckons them to return to the stream where they were spawned. How do salmon know to do that? Some say that it's instinct, but try to find your own way to some specific place without directions, by instinct alone. It is one of the great mysteries of life.

And so it is with ships; they, too, seem to follow a similar path. They are "born" near the water and head for the sea. During their "life" some become famous, others fall into anonymity. Then, there are those that are destined for tragedy, never returning from their voyages. Such a ship was the *Growler*, a submarine that was launched just before the beginning of World War II.

The ceremony went badly; Lady Luck didn't attend the launching. The bottle of champagne didn't break even on the third try. Finally, as *Growler* slid down the greased skids, a welder hurled the bottle and it broke. Lady Luck, it seems was late. People tried to make light of the incident, but the superstitious sailors didn't smile. They said it was an ill omen. If only we could read and understand the early warning signs.

To make matters worse, at the time of the launching an ancient whaling ship, the *C.W. Morgan* was being towed past the *Growler* to her final berth in Mystic Seaport. It was as if a ghost were beckoning.

During the short life of the *Growler* there were three captains. The first was Howard W. Gilmore, who died in a fusillade of enemy bullets along with a junior officer and a lookout. Gilmore was known to have said, "I don't want to hear anymore talk about a hard-luck ship."

Upon Gilmore's death, Arnold F. Schade, executive officer, became captain. His luck held, and he remained skipper for about a year and a half.

Thomas B. Oakely, Jr. turned out to be the unlucky third captain. In less than four months the *Growler,* which had been launched under a sign of darkness, disappeared forever, along with the entire crew of eight-six men. The exact cause is still a mystery. Perhaps Lady Luck deserted the *Growler* when Captain Oakley had most of the seasoned crew members transferred after he took command. He stated that he didn't want any commissioners aboard because he wanted men who weren't superstitious.

After the war ended, Robert A. Link, a former *Growler* crew member was one of three veterans who founded the U.S. Submarine Veterans, World War II. The first really large reunion was held in 1984 in Chicago. Remembering the lost submarine, we decided to gather each November 8, to hold a memorial service for those who had gone down with *Growler.*

George Wade, who had been on the bridge the night that Gilmore stepped into his immortality, offered his hometown of Litchfield, Texas. We didn't know that George had been diagnosed with terminal cancer. The town turned out in record numbers at the Veterans of Foreign Wars hall, and made the crew feel so welcome that we have returned again and again.

To keep the memory of *Growler* alive, we decided to write about our personal experiences while aboard the submarine. The stories that appear in this book were written by and about the men who served on the *Growler* who have a strong desire to leave a record for future generations of Americans of the sacrifices that were made by a group of young volunteers when our country was in grave danger.

We offer to you an opportunity to understand, first hand, an inside view of one of the fifty-two submarines that were lost during World War II.

WILLIAM HAGENDORN

Prologue

The history of World War II is made up of more than the great events that are forever etched in the world's memory. It is also the story of many individuals who served heroically in the war's various theaters. Some stories have been written in history books and military reports. Others are personal recollections shared at reunions and in newsletters.

Kangaroo Express: The epic story of the submarine Growler is a unique collection of previously unpublished material from the reports of a gallant submarine, the *Growler*, the personal recollections of its only surviving skipper, Adm. Arnold Schade (Ret.), and stories which first appeared in the *Kangaroo Express*, a newsletter named for the *Growler*'s nickname.

Skippers Howard Gilmore and Thomas B. Oakley, Jr. were among those who lost their lives in service to their country. The book is not only about the skippers, Schade, Gilmore and Oakley and the *Growler,* but all submariners who played such a major role in the defeat of the Japanese Imperial Navy in the Pacific, and of those since who preserve peace in the world today. They are all the real heroes! The living survivors of *Growler* have as their motto: "A Vow To Perpetrate Their Memory."

It has been my great privilege and pleasure to know Admiral Schade as a close personal friend. The personal recollections that he has shared with me during the course of writing this book will give readers a sense of the greatness of this man, and the dedication of the men with whom he served. Their stories must be preserved for future generations.

In 1912, two years before the onset of World War I, Woodrow Wilson was elected the twenty-eighth president of the United States. It was the same year that the SS *Titanic* sank on her maiden voyage after colliding with an iceberg resulting in the loss of 1,513 lives. Victor Herbert's *Naughty Marietta* was a popular American operetta performed in New York City.

And, on the 26th of February, Arnold Frederic Schade was born in Stamford, Connecticut, to a Dutch immigrant father and a Swiss-born mother.

Arnie, as he is known to his friends, was graduated from high school when he was fifteen and applied through his Congressman for admission to the Naval Academy at Annapolis, Maryland. Because so many other applicants failed their physicals, Schade had a choice between Annapolis and the Army Academy at West Point, New York. Without hesitation, Schade chose the Naval Academy. But he had a problem—he was only sixteen when he received the appointment, and he had to be seventeen to enter. Fortunately, his Congressman was able to keep the appointment open until Schade's seventeenth birthday and he entered the Naval Academy in August 1929.

Midshipman Schade was graduated from the Naval Academy in 1933. It was during the Depression and President Franklin Roosevelt (assistant secretary of the Navy in 1913) attended the graduation where he explained that the nation could not afford a full naval force and that only the top half of the class would be commissioned. Schade was in the top half of his class so he was among those receiving a probationary commission as ensign. All new ensigns were on probation for two years and could not marry during that time. However, there was no prohibition on falling in love.

While awaiting for his first cruiser, the USS *Concord*, which was not yet in its San Diego port, Ensign Schade and a shipmate went on leave to Aqua Caliente, near Tiajuana, Mexico. There he met Rebecca Fiske, his future wife. Becky was dining in a restaurant with her father, a naval medical officer, and her mother. Luckily, Becky lived in San Diego where Schade's ship was based. As they dated when he was in port, the couple listened to the popular songs of 1933: "Smoke Gets in Your Eyes" and "Stormy Weather." It was true love; Arnie proposed and Becky said yes. They were married at the end of Arnie's two-year probation, on 15 June 1935.

In that year the SS *Normandy* crossed the Atlantic in one hundred seven hours and thirty-three minutes. Those remembering the year recall its melodies: "I Got Plenty of Nuttin'" and "It Ain't Necessarily So."

Peace wasn't necessarily so. With the seeds of World War II germinating throughout the world, those who had enlisted in the Navy would soon have their skills and bravery tested. Schade's professional training and leadership abilities were about to put to work on a submarine in the Far East—far from his home and family.

Life was more stressful on submarines than on other ships. Crew members have described it this way: "Imagine yourself crammed inside a cold, clammy, inescapable steel cylinder with eighty-five smelly souls for a period of thirty- to-sixty days. There is no fresh air—in fact there is a strong smell of combined body odors, diesel fumes, cooked food, stale air and lead-acid batteries. There is little space in which to get about and no days off. You are in constant fear of doom. But you volunteered for this job that pays very little."

Now add the ingredients of war: torpedoes and air strikes and the constant maneuvering to seek out or evade the enemy. Imagine being the skipper who gave the command to dive, knowing that it meant certain death for those left on deck.

Heroes are persons of great strength and courage who act for a higher purpose, without promise of reward or regard to their personal safety. *Growler* is an epic story of the heroes in World War II who manned the American submarines that contributed significantly to the defeat of an Imperial enemy.

This is a story that must be told because it reminds us of the gratitude we owe to the great men of the submarine force in World War II who risked everything for our country. While it is, in part, about one event, it must be recognized that the epic of *Growler* symbolizes a far larger picture of a man who also played an important part in our postwar world.

Schade's display of discipline, courage, character and leadership made him a credible counselor to presidents and high-level leaders who guided us through the Cold War. A decisive man with proven qualifications, during the Cuban Missile Crisis Admiral Schade was called upon on a daily basis by President John F. Kennedy for guidance of our naval operations in the Caribbean. No one knows better than Admiral Schade how close the world came to being involved in a third World War.

Even in retirement in 1971, after forty-two years of service to his country, Commander Schade did not cease to serve his countrymen. After moving to Port Charlotte, Florida, he gave the community the benefits of his rich leadership.

Schade has a strong sense of duty and closeness to his fellows. Even in those early days of World War II aboard a submarine in the Pacific, his men warmly referred to him as "Uncle Arnie." Indeed, even today, some fifty-five years later, those who served with him in the submarine force during World War II and after, still address him as "Skipper."

Arnie will have it no other way!

RICHARD J. LANIGAN

Remember the USS *Growler*

Remember....we never did forget,
    the days of battle,
the times of tears and sweat,
    and yet......

Wouldn't it be great
    if only for an hour, maybe two,
we all could return to yesteryear
    and again be part of the old *Growler* crew.

To shake the hands of those whose dreams
    never were fulfilled
and to hear the same old voices,
    that have so long been stilled.

Oh what a party there would be,
    everyone filled with good cheer,
I'm sure the tears would flow,
    more freely than the beer.

I know these are the dreams, of a man grown old
    and it can never really be.
But what a thrill if we could slip back
    to the year of nineteen forty-three.

If a chance like this came along
    you'd never pass it by,
So remember the *Growler* reunions
    a ghostly voice is calling for you and I.

WILLIAM F. "RADAR" HAGENDORN

Part One

Omens

1931–1939

Omens

Since the mid-1920s, it was a given that an apocalyptic clash between the Empire of Japan and the United States would occur, resulting in the ultimate destruction of one or the other. Some military leaders, such as Admiral Bradley A. Fiske, had predicted as early as World War I that Japan represented a great threat to the United States of America. General Billy Mitchell was court-martialed in 1925 for insubordination in his vigorous advocation of air power. He also thought that Japan was a threat to the United States. The disastrous attack on Pearl Harbor on 7 December 1941 proved him right.

U.S. Naval officer Schade was another military genius who had long expected that the United States was close to war with Japan. There were many omens in the years before 7 December 1941 attack on Pearl Harbor. Schade's first reflex was to contact his headquarters with a strong appeal for a boat. Aside from "I do," said at his wedding, the seven most important words in the life of Arnold Frederic Schade were: "Get me a boat," and later the dramatic command of his dying skipper, Howard Gilmore, to "take her down!"

Lieutenant Schade was assigned to the new fleet boat USS *Growler* as executive officer. His skipper was Lt.Comdr. Howard W. Gilmore. Later in the war, during a topside battle with a Japanese gunboat in the Pacific, Gilmore's command to Schade to take her down meant certain death for Gilmore, and made for an exceptional feat in Naval history.

When Rebecca Fiske first met her future husband, Ensign Arnold Schade, fresh out of the United States Naval Academy in Annapolis, Maryland in 1933, he told her matter-of-factly that, "the United States is headed for war with Japan." Arnold Schade, who had proposed to Rebecca Fiske almost immediately after meeting her, said he wanted her to know the risks of their relationship. This said two things about Arnold Schade. First, he was a decisive man who did not mince words. Secondly, he was honest about relationships. Surely he would never betray his trust. No one had to tell Rebecca Fiske that. And she was a "jewel" throughout his long and distinguished career as she kept in touch with all the wives and families while the men were at sea.

Rear Adm. (ret.) Arnold F. Schade.

Schade and Fiske were a perfect match from the beginning. Miss Fiske understood from the outset that it was a risk to marry a member of the military, as she came from a family rich in the Navy tradition. Miss Fiske's father was a U.S. Navy medical doctor officer when she met Arnold Schade. Her forefathers were Navy men going back to the time of Theodore Roosevelt. Becky was born in San Francisco, and was graduated from the University at Berkeley.

Rebecca Fiske and Ensign Schade were married in a double-ring ceremony on 15 June 1935. At the same time one of Schade's shipmates was married to the granddaughter of world-class contralto opera singer, Madame Schumann-Heinke, who sang at the wedding. After the wedding, Ensign Schade volunteered for the submarine force and was assigned to the Navy's submarine school in New London, Connecticut. The newly wedded Schades went from San Diego to New London, stopping in Detroit to buy a brand-new Ford.

Schade graduated from submarine school in 1937. During the Depression, it was very difficult to get promoted, but Schade showed promise and rose to the grade of lieutenant junior grade through competitive examinations that demonstrated his proficiency. In addition, Schade earned high grades for ship performance. A group of friendly officers suggested the submarine service. Schade said that although he didn't know a soul, "It sounded glamorous at the time."

After graduation from submarine school, Schade was assigned to an R-boat which carried thirty-six crewmen and three officers. Recognized as an officer with potential, Schade was trained on the new fleet boat that was the most modern submarine of its time. It carried a crew of eighty-five and had the latest sophisticated electronic equipment.

In 1937 Schade served on the first USS *Perch* which had been commissioned in late 1936. It had to be scuttled on 3 March 1942 after the Japanese had depth charged it between Java and Borneo. Schade said that the entire crew was able to escape but were interned by the Japanese for the duration of the war. The second *Perch* was commissioned on New Year's Day of 1944.

In 1939, Schade did graduate work at Annapolis. In that year he also served on the USS *Montgomery* and the USS *Dent*. Submariners were required to serve two years on surface ships before taking duty on a submarine.

Mandates

Emerging as a world power after its spectacular victory over the Russian Tsar's "invincible fleet" in the straits of Tsushmima in 1905, Japan was seen as a Pacific threat to the United States. Adm. Bradley A. Fiske was one who saw this early on, before World War I. To some World War II leaders, such as Adm. Chester Nimitz, men like Fiske had the clearest answer to Japanese aggression. To meet the threat, they developed "Plan Orange" which was to effect a quick decisive naval victory against Japan.

Japan, as an ally in World War I, was given former German Islands in the North Pacific Ocean under the provisions of the Versailles Treaty in 1920. The League of Nations supervised the administration of the territories which intended that these former colonies would be prepared for self government.

Despite the ban on fortifications on these territories, Japan secretly militarized their mandates in the Marshall and Caroline Islands. The Japanese built air and naval bases on Palau, Saipan, Yap, Truk, Ponape and Jaluit under the guise of "South Seas Trading Company" in 1922 as a commercial organization. While the United States suspected that such was the case, Japan did not allow inspection of the areas.

Amelia Earhart

About the same time that heroine Amelia Earhart mysteriously vanished on the last part of her flight in the Pacific Ocean, Schade was training on submarines that would be patrolling the area where she disappeared. Even though there was an extensive search by the U.S. Navy in the area of her last-known position, no actual trace of her was found, although many sightings and investigations, before, during and after World War II produced many rumors and theories of Earhart's demise. Among those rumors, still popular today, is that Earhart was on a secret mission for the United States government to find out what the Japanese were doing. If she were passing information to our government, then her facts would be useful to submariners operating in that area during the war.

The "Queen of the Air" was on the last part of her flight around the world when she vanished. With Earhart was Frederick Noonan, an experienced navigator and former Pan American pilot. Their plane was a twin-engine Lockheed *Electra* 10 E, which when fully fueled was capable of flying four thousand miles nonstop.

Earhart and Noonan had taken off from Lae, New Guinea on 2 July 1937 for Howland Island. In the early morning of 3 July, her last message was received. To many, Amelia Earhart and Fred Noonan became America's first casualties of World War II. With the plane's four-thousand-mile range, a detour to Saipan or the Marshalls was well within her range on the way to Howland Island.

An account by Vincent Loomis with coauthor, Jeffrey Ethell in their book *The Final Story* tells of the search for Earhart. "Despite a massive naval task force consisting of four thousand men, the aircraft carrier, *Lexington* with sixty-five airplanes, the battleship, *Colorado*, and other ships, joined in a search covering a quarter of a million-square mile area, approximating the size of the state of Texas, found nothing. The search lasted for three weeks and cost four million in 1937 Depression dollars. Never had there been such a extensive mass rescue attempt made for a single lost plane.

"In the ensuing years many theories on the fate of Amelia Earhart and Frank Noonan have emerged. One was that the United States, knowing that war with Japan was imminent, put Earhart and Noonan on a secret mission to find out what the Japanese were up to on their Mandated Islands in the Pacific. They were forced down by the Japanese and sent to Saipan who tortured them for information. Natives reported seeing a white woman and man resembling the description of Earhart and Noonan under Japanese guard. They said that the white man was beheaded and the white woman died of dysentery while in captivity.

"When the United States captured Saipan in 1944 clues popped up everywhere—a civilian *Electra* was found and later destroyed; Marines found pictures of Amelia Earhart on Japanese soldiers; a suitcase with a diary of Amelia Earhart and woman's clothes; and skeletons in a grave were rumored to be those of Earhart and Noonan. Their bones, as one story has it, were brought to Washington, D.C. and secreted in the National Archives."

Loomis quotes Fleet Adm. Chester W. Nimitz as saying before his death in 1966, "I want to tell you that Earhart and her navigator did go down in the Marshalls and were picked up by the Japanese." Even Congress was asked to investigate the case, but nothing has ever been done.

"Questions remain: Why did the United States launch such an expansive force during the Depression to find Earhart; why have all the questions regarding the clues not been properly answered: and, why has Congress refused to investigate? A detour from Lae to Howland via Truk would have totaled just about three thousand miles, well under the fuel endurance of the *Electra*!"

John Toland, in his book *The Rising Sun,* describes other prewar events that set the stage for the war in the Pacific that would soon involve the submariners, including Schade: United States immigration laws were further restricted by Congress's "Exclusion Act" which barred Japanese from the United States. Although an ally of the United States in World War I and a member of the League of Nations, it was becoming clear that troubles

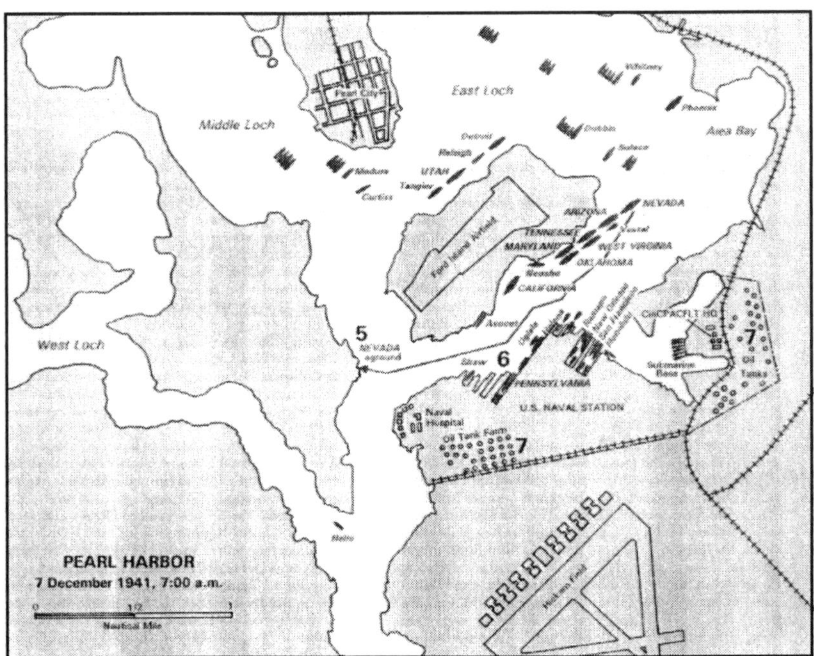

Diagram of Pearl Harbor as it was on the morning of December 7, 1941

between Japan and the United States were increasing. President Wilson, a major advocate of the League of Nations Treaty, which the United States Senate did not ratify, was calling on the Japanese Empire to return all Chinese territories conquered since the 1800s to China.

Toland notes that other events of 1937 included the Japanese escalation of the war in China on 25 July, when newly named Premier Prince Konoye sent more troops to China announcing a "New Order" in East Asia to protect Japanese lives. Japan seized Peking, Tientsin, Shanghai, Nanking and Hangchow. Generalissimo Chiang Kai-shek united with Communists Mao Tse-tung and Chou En-lai. President Roosevelt declared a quarantine against Japan. The sinking of the American gunboat *Panay* and three Standard Oil tankers by Japanese bombers on the Yangtze River in China, killing three people and injuring several others on 12 December, couldn't have been a clearer portent of the future.

Just prior to the Japanese attack, Lt. Harry J. Messick, who had helped commission the submarine tender *Fulton,* was on a shakedown cruise to Panama. "It was then on the morning of 7 December, the commanding officer announced that we were now at war with Japan."

Messick was born on 17 August 1908 and joined the U.S. Navy as an apprentice seaman in 1924 at the age of sixteen. He had served in the submarine USS S-41 on station with the Asiatic Fleet off China from 1932 to 1934. He was returned from Cavite to the United States in March 1941 to man the tender *Fulton,* which was then under construction at Mare Island, California.

Messick remembered that, "On the *Fulton* was gear for an advanced base including earth-moving equipment, underground storage tanks plus 2,300 fifty-gallon drums of high-test gasoline. After establishing the base and a fueling pier we named the Nicaragua base Sun-Ova-Beach. A second trip was made but this time to the Galapagos Island where we delivered steel mats, gasoline and, of course, the men to run it."

In the August 1988 issue of the *Kangaroo Express* Messick wrote: "We returned to San Diego to pick up a draft of recruits and then proceeded to Pearl Harbor where I saw a ship that I had once sailed on, the USS *Oglala,* which was now capsized alongside the pier. The rest of the harbor was a sea of oil littered with sunken and damaged ships."

Warriors

The Pacific Submarine Fleet was in good hands during World War II. From top to bottom, competent men made the submarine force a major reason for the Empire of Japan's defeat. When, at 11:05 P.M. on 14 of August 1945, Admiral Nimitz ordered all units to cease hostile operations he later compared submariners with the best. He wrote, "As British airmen are credited with saving Britain in those critical days after Dunkirk, so our gallant submarine personnel filled the breach after Pearl Harbor, and can claim credit, not only for holding the line, but also for carrying the war to the enemy." The chain of command was comprised of able leaders but more importantly by the men in the front line who manned the boats.

Following the attack by the Japanese on Pearl Harbor, President Franklin D. Roosevelt named Adm. Ernest Joseph King Jr. (1878–1965) to the post of commander in chief, United States Fleet, and chief of Naval Operations, replacing Admiral Stark. Roosevelt saw the value of submarines as early as World War I when he was assistant secretary of the Navy. King was graduated from the United States Naval Academy in 1901 and began his career as a midshipman in the Spanish-American War of 1898.

During his career, King became an expert on surface, submarine and air warfare. In 1933 he became a rear admiral. Under King, naval air power reached its greatest strength through his leadership. In 1941 he was promoted to admiral and commander of the Atlantic Fleet.

As commander in chief, he directed the greatest naval fleet in history. He was also chief of naval operations and held both assignments until after the war. King was the only officer in American naval history to hold both posts. He represented the Navy on the Joint Chiefs of Staff and on the combined Chiefs of Staff committee. In 1944 King was promoted to the newly created rank of Fleet Admiral.

Admiral King, in turn, appointed former submariner Admiral Chester Nimitz (1885–1966) to replace Admiral Kimmel as commander in chief, Pacific Fleet. Nimitz was graduated from the U.S. Naval Academy in 1905 and began his career in submarines.

Between 1911 and 1914, the New London Ship and Engine company began building submarine diesels. The first of these diesel-powered boats was placed into commission by young Chester Nimitz who had previously commanded gasoline-powered boats. Nimitz soon became the Navy's leading authority on diesel submariners.

Recognizing Nimitz's talents, superiors promoted him swiftly through the ranks. He became lieutenant, skipping the junior-grade rank due to his outstanding abilities. As rear admiral, his flagship during the mid-1930s, was the doomed USS *Arizona*.

Admiral Nimitz assumed command at Pearl Harbor on 31 December 1941, just three weeks after the fleet had been almost completely disabled by the Japanese attack. Tradition had the commander in chief's flag hoisted on a battleship. But because all the battleships at Pearl Harbor were disabled or sunk, Admiral Nimitz had his CINCPAC flag placed on the submarine USS *Grayling*. This was to prove symbolic when the U.S. submarine fleet became a major cause for the defeat of Japan. It was symbolic because as a former submariner Nimitz knew that the submarine force was his first line of offense, which it turned out to be.

Nimitz slowly rebuilt the United State's strength in the Pacific. As commander of the combined Pacific Fleets he directed Navy and Marine forces. Despite Congressional and media pressures in the early days of the war, Admiral Nimitz would not commit to any major attacks before United States's forces were fully restored to pre-Pearl Harbor strength. The admiral's calm assurance of final victory did much to rally the U.S. Navy's faith in its own powers and abilities.

Despite significant disagreements with General MacArthur, Nimitz developed much of the island-hopping strategy on key islands on the path to Japan. In particular, Nimitz and MacArthur clashed on the conduct of operations on Guadalcanal. In a major conflict between the two concerning the Philippines, President Roosevelt intervened on the side of MacArthur. Admiral Nimitz was promoted to fleet admiral in 1944 and signed for the United States at the Japanese surrender ceremonies on board USS *Missouri* in Tokyo Bay on 2 September 1945.

Admiral Nimitz's son, Chester William Nimitz, Jr., served in the submarine force throughout the war. As commander of the USS *Haddo*, father pinned son with a Silver Star for bravery against the enemy. In May 1942,

Admiral Nimitz appointed Robert Henry English to succeed Tommy Withers as commander of Submarines Pacific at Pearl Harbor. Unfortunately, seven months later, on 20 January 1943, English was killed in a plane crash on his way to visit the submarine support facilities at Mare Island, near San Francisco. Admiral King ordered the Bureau of Personnel to name Rear Adm. Charles Andrews Lockwood (1890–1967) to replace English.

Lockwood graduated from the U.S. Naval academy in 1912. He was the right man, becoming the outstanding submarine expert in commanding the Pacific Submarine Fleet from early in 1943 until the end of the war. Lockwood had served on many of the earlier submarines. His first command was the A-2 at Cavite, Philippine Islands in 1914, and he spent most of World War I in Manila Bay, commanding the aging *Adder* (A-2) and *Viper* (B-1). During the closing days of the war he was transferred to the Submarine School in New London. Thereafter he held various commands in the Far East. In the late 1930s, before World War II, he had considerable influence designing the new *Tambor*-class fleet boat.

Declassified U. S. Navy photograph

Charles A. Lockwood

In late March 1942, Admiral King had ordered Lockwood to Perth as commander Submarines Southwest Pacific (Asiatic Fleet). In May of 1942 Lockwood was promoted to rear admiral and commander of the Allied Naval Forces. When he replaced English at Pearl Harbor, he would come to play a key role in the victory over the Japanese Empire. The forces that Lockwood commanded would sink more than a thousand enemy ships and damage over five hundred more, a major cause in Nippon's defeat.

On 10 December 1941, Rear Adm. John Wilkes was the commander of the Submarine Asiatic Fleet in the Philippines. The Asiatic Fleet had participated in the defense of Java and the eventual evacuation of the Philippines to Fremantle, Australia. Wilkes set up headquarters in Perth with an operational fleet of nineteen submarines. In April 1942 Lockwood replaced Wilkes in Fremantle's demoralized command.

Capt. Ralph Waldo Christie, a major participant in the development of the Mark XIV torpedo, was, in 1942, commander of most of the Atlantic's

S-boats, under the command of Admiral Edwards. Christie was selected to relocate some of Atlantic Submarine Fleet to Brisbane, Australia. This decision by Admiral King to boost the Pacific Fleet was to help defend Australia against an anticipated Japanese invasion.

Arriving on the 15 April 1942, Christie established a submarine base— New Farm Wharf. When Lockwood replaced English, Christie, in turn replaced Lockwood at Perth-Fremantle, but was subsequently recalled to the United States to work on the torpedo problem. As will be more fully explained in the chapter on torpedoes, the reason they didn't work was because of the angle of the shot and a faulty "pistol." There was not much Christie could do so he was sent back to Fremantle and promoted to rear admiral in early 1943. Toward the end of the war in December 1944, Christie was abruptly relieved of his command at Admiral Kinkaid's request. No reason was given but it seems that Christie had ruffled many a feather.

Rear Adm. James Fife, Jr., who had replaced Christie in late December 1942 in Brisbane, again replaced Christie in Fremantle in late December 1944. Fife had been Wilkes's chief of staff in Manila when the Asiatic Fleet was evacuated to Fremantle in the early days of the war. Fife was a 1918 graduate of the Naval Academy. A long time submariner who had commanded the fleet boat *Nautilus* and the Submarine School, was a strict disciplinarian.

Lieutenant Commander Schade reported to, and had a very high regard for, Fife. Schade considered him tough but fair.

The reason that the U.S. Pacific Submarine Fleet was so effective was that it had an outstanding leadership and competent submarine commanders such as Schade.

There were political leaders, the military warriors, but the real heroes were those on the front line. This book is about the heroes who led and manned the boats such as the *Growler*—they were the true heroes—this was a real epic!

Part Two

Growler

1942–1944

Fleet Boat

Growler was a fleet boat. Unlike older submarines that were smaller and slower, unable to keep up with the fleet, fleet boats had more speed and endurance—hence the name "fleet boat." Mostly they were of the *Tambor*-class prototype which had many advantageous features over the many older boats in the Asiatic and Pacific Fleets. They could travel ten thousand miles without refueling.

By July of 1940, it was obvious that a major war was coming. Congress voted to spend four billion dollars to create a "Two Ocean Navy." The bill included more money for the construction of the new *Tambor*-class fleet boats. Prototypes had been developed in the early 1930s, and numbers of them were in service by 1941.

The Navy expanded submarine construction facilities at Electric Boat Company in Groton, Connecticut, and the Navy shipyards at Portsmouth, New Hampshire, and Mare Island off the California coast. At the outbreak of World War II there were fifty-five submarines in service. These formed the backbone of the United States fleet assigned to the Pacific Ocean.

According to Keith Wheeler in *War Under the Pacific*, "The new fleet boats were larger and more powerful than earlier submarines. They were 312 feet in length and sixteen feet in diameter. They displaced 1,525 tons

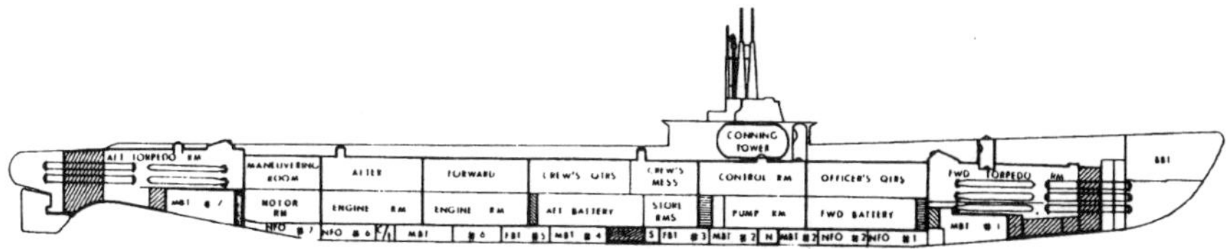

A cutaway diagram of a "fleet boat" similar to USS Growler *(SS 215).*
See the inside back cover for more detail.

on the surface and had a cruising range of 10,000 miles with supplies for sixty days. It had ten twenty-one-inch torpedo tubes and armed first with three-inch or four-inch guns and after 1942, five-inch deck guns. With four 1,600 horsepower diesel engines it could cruise 20 knots (23 mph) on the surface and 9 knots (more than 10 mph) under water. The approved operating depth was 200 feet, but often went to 300 feet or more during intensive depth charge attacks. They could dive to periscope depth (63 feet) in less than a minute. The fleet boat could stay underwater for 48 hours at reduced speed, powered by 252 storage battery cells and 1,100 kilowatt generators. The batteries would be recharged at night on the surface. They carried twenty-four torpedoes which could be launched from six foward tubes and four aft.

"The submarine's control room housed the main systems for diving and surfacing. Levers at the hydraulic manifold controlled vents the tops of the ballast tanks which when opened, allowed air to escape as it was replaced by tons of water rushing in through flood ports in the bottom.

"Above the hydraulic manifold was the "Christmas Tree," a panel of red and green lights that showed the status of every hull opening. Green all around meant that the submarine was watertight and ready to dive. Two wheels at the diving station changed the angle of the bow and stern planes, the horizontal fins used to maintain depth. The trim manifold controlled the amount of water in the trim tanks to keep the boat level, while the air manifold regulated high pressure air used to empty the tanks when surfacing. Below the control room, the pump room was filled with machinery for the compressed air, hydraulic refrigeration and air conditioning systems.

"The boat's command center was the conning tower, a tiny auxiliary/ hull above the main pressure hull, reached by a hatch from the control room. Here the skipper could draw on data obtained from the boat's eye and ears—periscope, radar and sonar.

"The fleet boat was manned by seventy-five enlisted men and eight officers. All submariners were volunteers—the cream of the Navy! Early in the war, one-third of the crew was rotated after each run and later in the war back to the states so that a new boat wouldn't be manned by a green crew.

"In the course of World War II, 250 U.S. submarines saw duty in the Pacific. There were 190 boats that sank at least one major Japanese vessel, in all 201 warships for a total of 540,192 tons including one battleship, four large aircraft carriers, four small carriers, three heavy cruisers, eight light cruisers, forty-three destroyers, and twenty-three large submarines. And that was the least of it.

"Of vastly greater importance in the war's outcome, the submarines would send to the bottom 1,113 Japanese ships of more than 500 tons each for a staggering tonnage of more than five million, only a million less than the entire prewar Japanese Merchant Fleet.

Growler (SS-215) was launched on a grey and gloomy Thanksgiving Day, 20 November 1941, by Electric Boat Company in Groton, Connecticut. It was sponsored (christened) by Mrs. Robert L. Ghormley, wife of Vice Admiral Ghormley, and commissioned 20 March 1942. Lieutenant Commander Howard W. Gilmore, the submarine's first skipper, second in command, Executive Officer Lieutenant Arnold Frederic Schade, and crew were present.

According to a story in the *Kangaroo Express,* corroborated by Schade, the ceremony didn't go well and some nervously joked that this could be an ill omen. The bottle of champagne didn't break when swung by Mrs. Ghormley on either the first or second try. Finally, someone seized the bottle and threw it at *Growler,* but it bounced off, still unbroken. As *Growler* was sliding down the ways a welding inspector picked up the bottle and hurled it like a football. This time it broke.

The year 1941 did indeed end on a grim note. Japan had attacked the United States without warning or with a declaration of war. Germany and declared war on the United States the following day. The United States responded by declaring war on the Axis, with but one dissenting vote in Congress.

But there were lighter moments to remember as well. Submariners and the girls they were to leave behind recall such popular songs in 1941 as: "Deep in the Heart of Texas," "I Don't Want to Set the World on Fire," "Chattanooga Choo-Choo," and, "I Got It Bad and That Ain't Good."

William R. "Little Stinky" Davis served on the old S-45 before participating in the commissioning of the new fleet boat *Growler* in early 1942.

He remembers that the S-boats were broken-down and relatively ineffective. Their habitability was terrible. The periscopes vibrated too much and the fire control of torpedoes was crude and too much a matter of by guess-and-by-God. S-boats, as described by Capt. William J. Ruhe USN (ret.) in his book *War in the Boats*, were "rusty old sewer pipes." Nevertheless, they were viewed by the Australians as their first line of defense against a Japanese invasion. They felt that these S-boats that had fled from the Philippines after the Japanese attack would be a deterrent and discourage the Japanese from landing their forces in Northern Australia.

"So it was with some pleasure that Davis was assigned to the *Growler.* The new fleet boats were much more reliable and habitable. They had air conditioning, bunks with mattresses, several heads, and enough water for occasional showers. There was little vibration and hardly any leakage of seawater. According to Captain Ruhe, he liked best the analog fire control computer. The fleet boats also had fifty percent more speed on the surface which would assure a greater success in night surface attacks."

During trials going down the Thames River in Connecticut, Davis recalled that "near the end, Commander Gilmore was on the bridge with an Electric Boat engineer running on *Growler*'s four main engines making 18-21 knots, when the command 'rig out the bow planes'—full dive, was given. Down went the boat with the main induction closed. The suction tore off the doors in the aft battery. They went into the engine room. The conning hatch was closed. When the boat went under there

Declassified U. S. Navy photograph

A group of fleet boats nestled next to their tender.

was a big suction in the boat before the engines shut down. Commander Gilmore and the engineer went up periscope shears and got wet before the boat came back up. COB C.T.M. Davenport saved our ass. He had been an Electric Boat employee and had come out of retirement to our boat."

In a prewar book titled *How Japan Plans to Win,* Kinoaki Matsuo, a Japanese agent equivalent to the U.S. Office of Strategic Services (now the CIA), had this to say about American submariners:

"The submarine is a very unhealthy weapon. Step inside, and though you may be able to stand the ventilation, your eyes are confronted to a world of darkness. The sub is so narrow and oppressive, it seems as though you are being pushed into the internal organs of the human body, and that God has opened a living Hell before your very eyes.

"In America, they lay emphasis on the ideal of individual rights. They will have trouble obtaining submarine crews, and there is no reason to expect an excellent fighting spirit from these men."

What a wrong assessment that was!

Torpedoes

Torpedoes were the essence of the fleet boat.

With his famous words from August 1864, "Damn the torpedoes. Full steam ahead," Admiral David G. Farragut won fame during the American Civil War in the Union's victorious battle of Mobile Bay. During World War II, prior to 30 September 1943, that may have not been an heroic order by Japanese warship commanders because before that date the United States Submarine Fleet was experiencing serious mechanical failures with duds and premature detonations of their torpedoes.

Submarine commanders were frustrated with knowing that they had made sure hits that didn't score on their targets. It was a problem that they were struggling with since the outset of World War II when a new secret torpedo, the Mark XIV, was introduced. Many skippers lost the confidence of their crews because of the many misses. Some discouraged captains asked to be assigned to other duties.

One submariner—Schade, the executive officer of the *Growler*—was well aware of the problem and had resolved it by arming the torpedoes for detonation upon impact. This resulted in the sinking three destroyers at Kiska on the Fourth of July, 1942. The new torpedo, the Mark XIV steam torpedo, was armed with a new Mark VI exploder which was, at that time, the state of the art.

The Mark XIV was a missile over twenty feet long and twenty-one inches in diameter. It had a TNT warhead which was detonated by the Mark VI exploder or "pistol." It was propelled by steam generated in an internal heat and water device that ran a turbine within the cylinder, which in turn drove the torpedo's two propellers. The torpedo weighed more than 3,000 pounds including over 500 to 668 pounds of TNT in the warhead. It was programmed to arm 360 yards from the sub and it could be programmed for two speeds, one over fifty miles per hour for over two and a half miles, or over five miles at thirty-six miles per hour. It was designed to run under a ship rather that hitting it head on. The idea was that a metallic steel hull generated a magnetic field which would activate the detonator. The reason for this was that an explosion under a ship does a great deal more damage than a direct hit. Only they didn't work, according to Pacific Submarine Fleet Commander, Vice Adm. Charles A. Lockwood.

Ralph Waldo Christie, Naval Academy Class of 1915 and one of the first graduates of the Submarine School at New London, helped develop the Mark XIV torpedo and the Mark VI Exploder in the 1920s. In the summer of 1922, Christie was shuttling between the Torpedo Lab at the Massachusetts Institute of Technology, where he earned a master's degree in Engineering, and the Newport Torpedo Station. The Bureau of Ordnance (BUORD) appropriated $25,000 to the station with orders to produce an "influence" exploder on the highest possible priority. The work—known as Project g-53—was carried forward behind the highest veil of secrecy the Navy had ever created. Only a handful of people in the Bureau with a "need to know" were aware of the project, and none in the fleet, Lockwood said.

Because of failures of the torpedo early on in World War II, skippers were requesting permission to arm the torpedoes manually so that they would explode on impact. While Lockwood, a World War I submarine veteran, sympathized with his commanders, he would not grant their requests. Instead, he wanted to solve the problem himself. From his headquarters at Pearl Harbor, he oversaw tests which fired torpedoes at a submerged Cliff on Kahoolawe Island. He discovered that the solution had to do with angles—a 90-degree angle produced a dud; a 45-degree angle produced half the duds of the firings. But the real function of the exploder was due not solely to the angle. It had to do with a stronger arming ring which was being crushed on a 90-degree hit. By changing the angle of the shot, results were dramatic. After 30 September 1943, duds and premature detonations disappeared, according to Lockwood.

Then a new electric torpedo was introduced. While its speed was slower, 28 knots (over 32 mph), it became preferred because it had no tell-tale wake and kept its depth, unlike the steam torpedo which by the use of fuel would tend to rise before approaching its target.

At the end of 1942, United States submarines had sunk 138 merchant ships of almost 600,000 tons in spite of all the misses caused by faulty torpedoes. After solving the torpedo problem in late 1943 the sinking of enemy ships increased dramatically. In 1944 submarines sank 2,400,000 tons of merchant ships and 353,000 tons of warships including one battleship, seven aircraft carriers, ten cruisers, thirty destroyers, and seven submarines.

The torpedo problem had existed for more than half the duration of the war. Many submariners felt that if a reliable torpedo had been available from the beginning, the war would have been shortened. It was a tragic flaw whose cost to the United States war effort remains incalculable.

An article in the *Kangaroo Express,* May 1997, called "The Torpedo Special" outlines the "trials and tribulations and what you didn't know about torpedoes." The following story is reprinted with permission from the newsletter: "The inexcusable shortage of torpedoes during World War II stemmed from two basic causes. First Newport adhered to the mistaken idea that all effort should be placed on volume production. If spare parts were needed they could be procured by breaking down a complete torpedo. The second reason was every model had its own serial number even though Newport was using identical parts in different torpedoes. When all of the duplication of parts was reduced, suddenly the shortage disappeared.

"However, the lasting problem of production continued because Newport machinists refused to give up their crafting of beautifully made torpedoes, however faulty. Even incompetent workers were difficult to get rid of because of political pressure from Newport officials. The result was a tiny dribble of beautifully crafted torpedoes which were entirely unreliable.

"Those in power were aware of the multiproblem, but because of the closeness of the coming war, it was decided that there wasn't time to develop a new fish but would have to improve what they already had. The faulty fish were issued to combat submarines causing many lives to be lost needlessly.

"As early as 1937, a move to reopen the moth-balled Alexandria Torpedo Factory was defeated by the powerful Newport area politicians who preferred expansion of the Newport factory. Even with the pressures of war, Alexandria facility wasn't opened until Newport was assured of a factory expansion!

"But war pressure soon overwhelmed the military and they were forced to turn to the production-wise civilian companies such as Westinghouse, Western Electric, International Harvester and Pontiac Motors.

"Although America entered the war with armament far inferior to Germany or Japan, by 1945 the entire picture was reversed. Why? One of the main reasons was that the Axis powers didn't give a free rein to their scientists to develop newer weapons until it became too late to change the outcome of the war. But in America the development of new weapons was spurred on because of the late start. The Axis was complacent with their military lead.

"The best technical minds had already been recruited by civilian war-production companies. Now anyone who had some scientific training was offered a chance to enter an unknown field, offered a military deferment and a good paying position. Most were young, barely out of college, but spurred on with signs showing the ships sunk by U-boats that day. These highly motivated youngsters found themselves working alongside skilled men from whom they learned faster than they would in a schoolroom. After they had finished their day's work they would hold sessions to discuss ideas which resulted in improved and completely new models of torpedoes.

"Of course the military didn't like civilians interfering in their affairs as they thought only military men could develop weapons. When a test for the aircraft-launched homing torpedo FIDO was conducted in early 1943, a submarine was used as a target. The sub's skipper was irate as he asked 'what am I doing here when I should be in the war zone looking for the enemy?'

"The sub was trailing a 1,000-foot sea tape which gave the PBY an idea where the sub was located. But on that particular day the fog was very thick and the sea was so rough that the sea tape kept disappearing, but the pilot decided to launch anyway somewhere in the direction of the sub.

"Down 300 feet, the pinging torpedo could be heard in the sub, but the skipper still didn't believe that he could be found at this depth until he heard a loud 'kerplunk' as the torpedo plowed into the propeller guard, wedging fast. The sub limped back to port still holding the FIDO.

"Although the proud and complacent military once spurned assistance from industry, it finally learned that 'pride goeth before a fall.'

"The Bureau of Ordnance considered several locations for a test site for torpedoes before selecting Keyport, Washington. Test firing was done and then the spent torpedo was recovered and inspected to pinpoint any defects before it went into production. Not all projectiles could immediately be located so the Navy offered a $100 reward to any civilian returning a lost torpedo. For awhile one family made it a practice to motor out to the spent torpedoes before the retrieving vessel got there. Authorities finally became suspicious and upon investigation found six of the lost projectiles hidden under their house.

"Early experiments with sonar-guided torpedoes include one barely missing a ferryboat, or when one time a MARK-XVI broached and struck a retrieving vessel amidships. Another time one struck the side of a causeway, went airborne, leaping over a truck, then landed on the other side. One other tried to travel overland but it was tracked through a yard, where the corner of a house was missing! But it finally came to rest still hissing, just inches from the family automobile.

"Probably the funniest episode was when an obnoxious owner of the local marina would race around the torpedo range every time they were ready for testing.

"One day they were ready with a MARK-2T homing torpedo when the owner once again appeared in his high performance speedboat laughing and zigzagging all over the range. Suddenly the torpedo picked up the sound of his engine and headed straight for it. He swerved away just in time, then revved up his engine but the torpedo jumped right over his boat and no doubt scaring the wits out of him. He turned away and headed for home with the MARK-2T about fifty yards behind but gaining.

"Of course all he had to do was to turn off his engine and he would have been safe but he kept gunning it and got going so fast that he hit the beach at the Bangor ammo depot and went ass-over-teakettle with the MARK-2T right behind him. When he finally came to stop, a big Marine placed him under arrest, then threw him in the brig, broken arm and all.

"By the summer of 1942, Admiral Lockwood had reached the boiling point with the bureaucratic lack of action so he purchased 500 feet of netting from a local Australian fisherman. Working with Squadron Comdr. James Fife, he directed Skipper James Coe of the USS *Skipjack* to fire a torpedo at the net with a dummy warhead. The resulting hole in the net was twenty-five feet instead of the ten feet which was set on the torpedo. This was the first time a depth test was ever performed! The results were swift when Admiral King entered the fray.

"There had been only one test with a live warhead when two MARK-XIVs had been fired at the derelict "I" class sub resulting in the first fish missing and the second sinking of the old I-boat. No further testing was done.

"One of the main reasons for the depth real function was the pendulum was paced at a slight angle. Engineers said that it wouldn't have any noticeable effect. It did. When more explosive was added to the warhead, depth sensors were tested in still water but their figures didn't take into effect that the water pressure will drop as speed increases.

"Another overlooked, but important factor, was as time passed, the same MARK-XIV testing torpedoes were used over and over and the constant wear and tear caused by firing and recovery changed the test fish until they resembled something other than the original MARK-XIV.

"After all of the problems were solved, three different torpedoes were hailed as the most successful of World War II, namely the steam-driven MARK-XIV, the electric MARK-XVIII and the sonar-guided FIDO. The first submarine launched the acoustic MARK-XXVII torpedo, nicknamed CUTIE because of its diminutive size, it was in essence the FIDO or MARK-XXIV.

"Finally Western Electric Company began production of the MARK-XXIV and the first production model was delivered in March 1943. In May more than five hundred were on their way to submarine bases. The first lethal use was on 14 May, delivered by the British. Two sinkings resulted. The U-266 was destroyed by a Liberator on an Atlantic convoy and the other delivered by a Navy Catalina assigned to VP84 Squadron.

"The first U.S. Navy success came from the escort carrier USS *Santee*. A directive allowed the FIDO to be used only to attack an individual U-boat, so that, no survivors would reveal the new secret, tactics. Before the war ended FIDO became one of the most important weapons.

"In 1915, the U.S. Navy awarded a small contract to Sperry Gyroscope to develop an electric torpedo but the company abandoned the plan 1918 for lack of funding. The same happened at Newport with the lack of interest, as well as funding. However, a single technician labored on the idea almost, as a hobby which resulted in a prototype which failed. However, combining all the past knowledge another torpedo was made in 1928. This model represented thirteen years of development.

"With great expectations it was test-fired off Rhode Island. It sank! It lay on the bottom hidden from everyone for two years and Newport finally quit looking, but accidentally a passing ship snagged and recovered it. But Newport dropped the entire project in 1931.

"Because of the MARK-XIV problems, Newport looked at other models only as a stopgap, until the problem was solved. Knowing it was a tough problem, Newport handed the existing plans to Westinghouse but never followed through with some assistance or encouragement. Westinghouse decided to scrap the Newport plan in favor of a captured German model. It looked very easy to make a copycat but, the German manufacturers were as bad as Newport. Everything was a custom fit, and if a minor change was made, it became necessary to redesign the entire model. Sometimes parts that had been necessary in earlier models were left in even though their function was questionable.

"Finally, after being betrayed by Newport, Westinghouse redesigned the entire torpedo in the amazing time of three months and the BUORD had enough confidence to order 2,000 units. On 24 June the first test model was delivered. However, due to the lack of cooperation by the Navy because they didn't know how to deal with civilians as prime suppliers the end was still not yet in sight."

"By 1943, a test was set up but the results were a complete failure.

"Eli Reich was the test coordinator who was then the executive officer of the USS *Lapon.* They fired MARK-XVIIIs and found one problem after another.

"But by tradition Newport's attention continued to be focused elsewhere resulting in the demoralization of all concerned. Newport's attitude was 'NIH' (not invented here). Reich stated sabotage was maybe too strong a word, but Newport didn't budge one bit.

"Finally, Reich concentrated all efforts with Westinghouse and for six weeks they reconstructed and recalibrated the MARK-XVIII and before long, the new torpedo reached the Pacific war zone where the combat sub commander waited, but with some reluctance, for the new wakeless wonder.

"In August, 1943, Admiral Lockwood received a memo from Reich criticizing the BUORD and Newport. He suggested that some major changes be made. Lockwood forwarded the complaints to Washington. The admiral's letter could be blunt, even insulting and arrogant, but he also could write with masterful diplomacy. His tactful letter brought about swift change.

"Eventually, the MARK-XVIII became appreciated by the submarine force even though it traveled 12 to 15 knots slower than the steam driven MARK-XIV, but 'everyone was delighted with the feature of wakelessness which resulted in less depth-charging from the enemy.'

"In October 1943, the first MARK-XVIII confirmed sinking occurred and as the war progressed, each boat took a larger percentage of the electronics on war patrol.

"A final victory for the MARK-XVIII and Eli Reich occurred on 21 November 1943. As captain of the newly commissioned USS *Sealion,* two Japanese destroyers were sighted escorting a pair of battleships. In the *Sealion*'s torpedo tubes rested the new MARK-XVIIIs. After a three-hour chase Reich was still 3,000 yards away, too far away for a good shot but close enough for a try.

"He fired six torpedoes then turned for a stern shot. Now all the tubes were ready and he waited for an interminable time for the sound of a hit.

All of a sudden the sky lit up as if it were noon. The first salvo had hit the battleship *Kongo*, 31,000 tons, but one of the escorting destroyers moved into the path of the second salvo and was immediately sunk—it was the IJN *Urakaze*.

"The battleship moved on but its progress became slower and slower and at 0500, she rolled over and headed for the bottom. The *Sealion* had been trailing her all through the night and when she exploded Commander Reich must have felt a great satisfaction because it was all due to those questionable MARK-XVIIIs and done at an extra range which had a greater chance for a miss than a hit.

"Newport's technicians had been testing the troubled magnetic exploder using artificially created magnetic fields but they never developed sufficient data about magnetic fields created by the sea or the ships. Finally, under the constant urging by Admiral Christie, the Navy agreed to send the USS *Indianapolis* south to the equator to accumulate data about the magnetic effect on ships while nearer to the equator.

Declassified U. S. Navy photograph

Crewmen carefully lower a torpedo below decks during a resupply next to their tender.

"Using the newly developed 'electric eye' it was observed that as the dummy warhead passed below the ship it would trigger the mechanism quite successfully. But, as yet there were no live shots fired under battle conditions, Christie requested a scrap-hulk for testing. The chief of Naval Operations granted the request stipulating that the hulk, USS *Ericsson* would not be sunk! Further, if she was sunk accidentally or otherwise, Admiral Christie would be responsible for raising and repairing her!

"Christie, not surprisingly, declined the 'generous' offer.

"Someone said: 'If it is to be, it is up to me.'

"Therefore, the exploder was never subjected to a proper testing as had been the case with the MARK-XIV. Christie, after all those years, probably shrugged his shoulder and declared the exploder ready for combat, then under the most stringent security, began the production of the faulty, untested device. To insure secrecy all units were locked up, the BUORD issued dummy contact exploders allowing no visual contact. Because of the extreme secrecy surrounding the device, few submariners knew anything about them or their principal operation. Submarine commanders were advised to fire the fish a few feet away too low but never told why. Of course they correctly guessed that the Navy didn't want to talk about it, which they certainly didn't.

"It was very discouraging to the commanders to see their torpedo pass directly under an enemy ship without exploding. Of course the escort would then know the sub's location and begin dropping depth charges.

"Other times the torpedo would broach, then circle back to the sub, and in two known cases, sink them. The two subs known to have been lost from that problem were the *Tang* and the *Tullibee.*

"Eventually, the problems were solved by disconnecting the magnetic feature of the exploder and using the contact. The cause of the duds was solved by replacing a small ring with a heavier one, which cost less than one dollar.

"However, wars are won by the side that makes the least amount of mistakes. Consider this. The MARK-XXIV proved to be so effective against U-Boats that one hundred forty-two were fired but sank the amazing total of thirty-one U-Boats and damaged fifteen more.

"Fifteen months before the war came to an end a German rescue vessel discovered a MARK-XXIV floating in the English Channel.

"Although they were designed to sink after a run, they sometimes didn't. It was taken to German Air Force for evaluation. Their scientists concluded that it was an experimental torpedo with little potential. The German Air Force never told the Navy about the MARK-XXIV so they never discovered the reason why they were losing so many U-Boats. American subs fired one hundred-eight CUTIES (MARK-XXVII) resulting in twenty-four ships sunk and damaged. These results were due to the fact that the Japanese were caught by complete surprise and never developed counter measures for defense."

Get Me a Boat!

Schade was assigned to the USS R-12 in August of 1940. On 7 December 1941 while he was in Casco Bay near Portland, Maine, he heard about the Japanese attack on Pearl Harbor. Schade called headquarters with the demand to "Get me a boat!" When the USS *Growler* (SS 215), a new fleet boat was commissioned on 20 March 1942, Schade sailed as her executive officer. Shortly thereafter, the *Growler* headed for the Pacific under the command of Lt. Comdr. Howard W. Gilmore, of U.S. Naval Academy class of 1926.

Skipper Gilmore did not come up through the ranks as did most skippers. He had enlisted in the Navy as an ordinary seaman. He qualified by competitive examination for Annapolis and rose to command a submarine because of his abilities. One of his fellow officers thought Gilmore was born under an unlucky star. He had scars left by a peacetime incident in Panama, where thugs had attacked him and a fellow sailor, slashing his throat. Gilmore's first wife had died of a crippling disease and when he took *Growler* to war in the Pacific, his second wife was still unconscious from injuries suffered in a fall.

Schade remembers Gilmore as a strict, no-nonsense skipper. He went by the book and if someone goofed they knew it by the fact that Gilmore would not make a lot of it unless it was a monumental "snafu." He was a fair man.

While *Growler* was enroute to Midway, a ferocious sea battle was raging in the Coral Sea. For four days between the 4th and 8th of May, a task force under the command of Rear Adm. Frank J. Fletcher intercepted a Japanese Naval Force headed for Port Moresby in the Coral Sea. Port Moresby was an allied naval base in Southeastern New Guinea which Japan needed to invade Australia. The battle, which was fought by aircraft, was an important allied victory for it halted Japan's southward expansion and its threat to Australia.

Growler arrived off Midway on 6 June 1942, just as the first battle was ending. She was used as a beacon to guide United States's B-17 bombers to their targets. Unfortunately, the *Growler* was often mistakenly identified as a Japanese submarine and almost bombed.

According to numerous sources, Midway was the turning point of World War II. It was there the U.S. Navy scored its first major victory against Japan. One of Japan's most important objectives was to capture Midway Island and the Aleutian Islands, west of Alaska. Midway lies 1,250 miles northwest of Hawaii and halfway between the United States and Japan, a total distance of roughly 5,200 miles. Admiral Yamamoto thought that by seizing Midway, he could draw the Pacific Fleet away from Hawaii and win a decisive victory with his larger, stronger force.

During the Battle of Midway, *Fulton* was sent out to bring back the crew of the badly damaged carrier *Yorktown.* Messick recalled that "by the time we arrived, the cruiser *Portland* had already taken the *Yorktown's* crew aboard. While under way at 15 knots, the *Portland* transferred more than 2,300 men to the *Fulton* using a high line and the old coal bins for the transfer of the *Yorktown* survivors.

"Before we could transfer the wounded a submarine alert forced us to chop away the lines and disperse. Just over the horizon the *Yorktown* went with skeleton crew and the destroyer alongside her supplying power to the stricken vessel, were both torpedoed and sunk by a Japanese submarine," said Messick.

Later the *Fulton* and the *Portland* were able to rendezvous and complete the transfer of the wounded using the small boats of the *Portland.* This was done in a complete blackout at night which made it impossible to see more than a few feet. It was a very eerie feeling lowering stretcher slings to the boats below, guided only by the voices of the boat crew. The transfer was successfully completed and the Fulton safely returned all survivors to Pearl Harbor.

"Stinky" Davis, who was a member of the original crew of the *Growler,* said that "after the Battle of Midway, we went into its harbor. It was in shambles. One twin-engine Jap plane had been shot down east of Gooney Bird Hotel. The Pan Am hanger was full of holes and there were dead birds everywhere, with millions of blowflies.

"We ran aground and damaged the left prop. The strut was out of alignment. It always had made a 'rup-rup' noise after that."

Adm. Tsoroku Yamamoto (1884-1943) commanded the Japanese combined fleet at the time of the attack on Pearl Harbor. He was one of Japan's great admirals with a long and distinguished career in war and peace. Admiral Yamamoto opposed the policies that led to war with the United States. But, as a loyal military officer, he sponsored the planning that led to the Pearl Harbor attack as Japan's only chance for victory.

Before Pearl Harbor, the United States scored one of its greatest triumphs by cracking Japan's secret codes. This feat enabled Adm. Chester W. Nimitz, who had succeeded Adm. Husband E. Kimmel as Commander in Chief of the Pacific fleet, to know about Admiral Yamayoto's plans in advance.

On 4 June 1942, aircraft from the 100-ship Japanese Fleet began blasting Midway. Nimitz's Task Force commanders, Rear Admirals Frank J. Fletcher and Raymond A. Spruance, launched aircraft from the carriers *Enterprise*, *Hornet* and *Yorktown*. At the end of the two-day battle, Japan had lost four carriers and a third of its air arm—253 planes lost. An enemy submarine sank the crippled *Yorktown*. The Battle of Midway proved to be one of the most decisive victories in history. It ended Japanese threats to Hawaii and the United States.

Destroyer Row

It was like a shooting gallery—one, two, three ducks—all in a row! Bang! Bang! Bang! They're all dead. It was a spectacular beginning for the gallant *Growler* crew on her first combat action that Independence Day of 1942 when she put three Japanese destroyers out of commission. For Schade, this was his most memorable war patrol. He says it was those first sounds of torpedoes exploding on their targets that gave the war a reality.

Growler was destined to lead the attack to destroy the enemy in early 1942—and in the end to be doomed herself. Although Japan failed to seize Midway, it had bombed Dutch Harbor, Alaska. This was the site of an American Naval Air Base, which formed part of the continental air defense of the United States.

The bombing, shortly before the Battle of Midway, was meant to be a diversionary ploy to draw the United States Pacific Fleet away from Midway, but Admiral Nimitz was not fooled and ignored the Dutch Harbor attack. On 7 June 1942, Japanese troops occupied Kiska and Attu, at the western tip of the American Aleutian chain. "If Japan seizes Alaska, she can take New York. They won't attack Panama." So said Gen. William E. Mitchell many years earlier. It is still a mystery why the Japanese never did attack the Panama Canal where United States warships passed through in World War II to defeat Japan. Japanese submarines certainly had the capability and did indeed make several attacks on the west coast of the United States in early 1942. Japanese submarines had a range of sixteen thousand miles.

When Russia offered to sell Alaska to the United States in 1867, Congress hesitated—it was too far north and the asking price of $7,200,00 was just too much. It was considered an extravagant folly of then Secretary of State William H. Seward (1801–1872) which was called "Seward's Ice

Box." Imagine what history might have been without America's forty-ninth state.

After the Battle of Midway, *Growler* was directed to attack Japanese forces in the Aleutians. The following is taken from Skipper Gilmore's "War Patrol Report," written by Schade (as executive officer, he wrote all reports):

20 June 1942:

    0915   Departed Pearl Harbor enroute Midway. Conducted Daily training dives and drills enroute. Fired four (4) rounds 3"/50 target ammunition during drills on June 21, 1942.

21 June, 1942.

    0729   Latitude 23°24' N., longitude 162°00' W., sighted B17; exchanged recognition signals; did not dive (Plane #1).

    1255   Latitude 24°08'N., Longitude 163°17' W., sighted B17; exchanged recognition signals; did not dive. (Plane #2)

24 June 1942:

    0600   Arrived Midway. Fueled to capacity. Charged torpedoes for MTB's.

    1035   Reported for duty to Comtaskfor 8 by despatch.

    1430   Departed enroute Dutch Harbor. Made trim dive after clearing harbor. Conducted daily training dives and drills enroute. Fired six rounds 3"/50 target ammunition on 25 June 1942.

As the distance from Pearl Harbor to Midway is 1,275 miles, *Growler* averaged a speed of almost thirteen miles per hour during the 93-hour trip. The report continues:

27 June 1942:

    0043   Received NPN Fox #489—operation order. Changed course to proceed to patrol area

30 June 1942:

    0130   Entered Amchitka Pass 0550 Entered assigned patrol area, forty-five miles East North Head Kiska.

About 196 hours elapsed in getting from Midway to the patrol area, which was 1,445 miles distance. Traveling submerged during the day and on surface at night *Growler*'s average speed was over seven knots an hour.

On the Fourth of July, big fireworks were in the making. In anticipation of battle, one of executive officer Schade's responsibilities was to supervise the arming of the torpedoes. At the time, the submarine force was experiencing problems with their torpedoes and they were required to arm them with the new secret "pistol" which didn't work. Schade knew better and armed the torpedoes for contact detonation. Schade never told the skipper, so it is questionable that Gilmore ever knew. A major function to an

USS *Growler* (SS 215) First Run Muster

Enlisted Men
Bialko, Daniel
Bloss, Fred
Bromley, James
Bucci, Anro
Carico, Donald
Coggin, John
Creeger, Harold
Cook, William
Davenport, James
Davis, William
Dynarski, Alexander
Farmer, William
Feit, Carl
Finnley, Carl
Forest, Milton
Gordon, Allan
Griffin, William
Griffith, Clyde
Grossman, David
Hamlett, Ivan
Hammond, Levon
Havens, Paul
Henthorn, Howard
Hilsabeck, Delbert
Hirst, Holroyd
Hollingsworth, Bardell
Holmes, Joseph
Hunt, Charles
Jenes, Euin
Johnson, Eddie
Jones, Bender
Jones, Dean
Jones, James
Jordan, Everett
Kelley, Warren
Kight, Delbert
Lantis, Wayne
Lassiter, Norman
Lynch, Timothy
Lynn, Charles
Manske, Robert
Mayer, Joseph
McCabe, Leonard
McFall, Louis
Mills, Ralph
Morgan, Richard
Morrison, Delmar
Pearce, William
Peart, Alvis
Prophet, John
Pugh, Jake
Richmond, Frank
Robison, William
Seletnik, Stanislaus
Schultz, Charles
Schweida, Charles
Soczek, William
Stephens, Hustin
Taylor, Billy
Triplett, Harold
Ullrich, Arthur
Vucovican, William
Wade, George
Wagner, William
Wandell, John
Weymouth, Milton
Wiles, William

Officers
Lt Cmdr Gilmore, Howard
Lt. Schade, Arnold
Lt. jg Cunningham, John
Lt. jg Currie, John
Lt. jg Davis, Landon
Lt. jg Pugh, Douglas

executive officer is take on the main details of the boat so that the skipper can concentrate on the big picture such as destroying the enemy.

There are no absolutes in war, but until Independence Day 1942, it was axiomatic that submarines were to stay clear of destroyers. Subs could attack merchant vessels, transports, aircraft carriers, cruisers, battleships or anything else that floated, but not destroyers. Destroyers were the deadly enemies of submarines.

A destroyer is the one of the smallest seagoing combat ships. It is about three- to- four-hundred feet in length and displaces approximately from one- to- four-thousand tons. Destroyers are used to protect other ships and to picket certain areas. They are long-range, high-speed, hard-hitting warships. "Tin Cans," as they are called because of their light steel hulls, can reach speeds of more than forty miles an hour. Destroyers, armed with torpedoes in tubes on deck, multipurpose five-inch guns and depth charges, are a lethal threat to submarines.

Schade remembers that *Growler* stealthily crept into Kiska's foggy harbor at five o'clock in the morning to see what the Japanese had there. With great skill and ingenuity, using every device at his command, Gilmore made his way into the enemy's hiding place. As *Growler* prowled along the rocky coast she came abreast a small cove and the skipper found himself eyeball-to-eyeball with three Japanese ships. At cautious intervals, Gilmore raised the periscope long enough for a quick look. He was almost within a point-blank torpedo range when the veiling mist broke enough for Gilmore to realize that he was staring down the throats of three new 1,700-ton destroyers of the Japanese Imperial Navy's *Fubuki* class. All three were riding at anchor, comfortably berthed and apparently happily content with the fog's protection, according to reports.

Rather than trying to pick off the destroyers one by one, Gilmore decided to go after all three with a single salvo. In what ranks as one of the war's most remarkable assaults, within a thousand yards Skipper Gilmore carefully trimmed his position and fired. The jolt of the torpedoes launching on their first war patrol ran through the boat and the crew knew that they were in a battle. A second deeper and stronger shock came back to the *Growler* a few seconds later. Only Gilmore at the periscope saw geysers rise up out of the water and a destroyer, ripped into by the unsuspected fury of 600 pounds of TNT, went down like a rock.

As Schade tells the story:

"When the Japs were driven off, we were told to go into Midway and supply support for all the PT boats, and then Admiral Nimitz called (Gilmore was still skipper, but somehow they always dealt with me as the exec) and said he was going to send us up to the Aleutians because the Japs have landed there in force. We want you to get up there and raise a little hell. So we took off for Kiska. We found that the Japanese had landed at Kiska immediately after the battle of Midway, and had taken it over and were about to come down into the continental U.S. We got there at five o'clock in the morning. I remember it very distinctly. We had never had much use for radar at that point, but at the beginning of the war it was a little blessing that we had. Kiska has a beautiful harbor and a nice little enclosure. And, outside the enclosure were three Japanese destroyers, brand-new Japanese destroyers. So we backed off and fired one torpedo at each. Boomp. Boomp. Boomp. Two of them went down immediately and the third was out of the war forever.

"So we were heroes. We were told to go to Dutch Harbor and refuel and c'mon back and, we were given the royal treatment by Nimitz and everyone else."

The enemy destroyers were *Arare Maru*, *Kasumi Maru* and *Shiranuhi Maru*. The Japanese had returned *Growler's* fire with torpedoes of their own. As the Japanese torpedoes swished by the *Growler* on both sides, she dove deep. It took considerable jockeying to get turned around and to head out to sea again, but despite the Japanese depth bombing attack followed by an aerial bombing attack, *Growler* got away.

So it was an incredible feat that on that Independence Day an American submarine, in such fog-bound waters, blew up three Japanese destroyers in as about as many minutes. While the report stated the fifth of July, it was the fourth of July in the United States of America. *Growler* patrolled Kiska area for the next few days with several encounters with the enemy:

6 July 1942:

0200	Stood in toward Kiska Harbor on surface; visibility 1 mile.
0540	Submerged and stood toward scene of attack; visibility about 2 miles.
0741	Sound picked up whining noise bearing 210° true. Visibility was low. Had just completed periscope observation about 0738. Had sighted nothing. On observing now, sighted patrol vessel (contact #5) distance 1000 yards headed directly for <u>Growler</u>. Swung away to course 030° T. Apparently undiscovered. Heard no screws but did hear pinging, which continued.
0902	Pings now bearing 230°. Picked up screws on bearing 285° true, (contact #6). Screws sounded like those of patrol vessel. Both patrol vessels trailed <u>Growler</u> until 1130. Kept retiring northeast until
1212	Changed to South in attempt to run around patrol vessels and close Kiska. Evaded them.

1626	Visibility now so poor that no observation of Kiska Harbor possible. Retired to North.
1910	Surfaced; visibility zero.
2001	Heard eight (8) explosions in direction of Kiska Harbor.
2105	Sound picked up pings and screws bearing 120° true and 302° true, (contact #7 and #8). Sounded like patrol vessels. Manned guns and closed each bearing in turn - never sighted vessels. Heard pings and screws intermittently until 2240.

7 July 1942:

0200	Proceeded down Eastern edge of 100 fathom bank, intending to approach Kiska from East, visibility 2 miles.
0713	Submerged, course 260° T.
0715	Heard pinging, bearing 270° T. (Contact #9). Different from patrol boats, maybe a destroyer. Finally all pings were directly on Growler. Could see nothing in periscope. Screws heard later were not like a patrol boat.
0738	Reversed course. Started evasive tactics.
0746	Heard depth charges to Westward.
1750	Sighted heavy destroyer, (Contact #11), bearing 0° T. Lying to or cruising at slow speed, course East, range 2000 or less yards. GROWLER headed 090° T., submerged. Believed GROWLER was sighted first as visibility was better to Southward.
1752	DD headed directly for GROWLER, range 1500 yards or less. Speed 15 knots or more (bow wave nearly to forecastle). Started to fire but decided it would be a waste of torpedoes. Range estimate was poor; gyro angles would have been 120° or more. Big spread would have been required. Furthermore, he was headed astern (angle on bow 5° port). Went ahead full and started for 250 feet.
1757	First charge of eleven (11) depth charge barrage. Swung left to get tail away. First charge 200 to 300 yards away on port quarter; remainder all astern. Nearest estimated 100 yards. Last dropped at 1800. Started evasive tactics running North as much as possible. Damage as follows: 1. Three (3) lights (not shock mounted) broke in after torpedo room. 2. Stern planes operate jerkily. 3. Propellers make a clicking noise at speeds over 2 knots.
1842	Pinging weak but in our direction.
1852	Pinging louder, coming closer. Definitely on GROWLER; bearing 170° T. Created another knuckle and got behind it.
1854	DD getting close, about 10° on starboard quarter. When bearing was 160° relative and screws of destroyer speeded up, swung away at full speed; started rigging in QB sound gear.
1858	First of three charges.

1859	Last charge.

1859   Last charge.
All went off and to starboard, nearest estimated at 50 yards. Continued evasive tactics. Failed to get QB rigged all the way in. It was damaged but still usable. Continued to hear screws trailing vessel/vessels or new noises on ship until 2204.

2232   Made battle surface. Retired on 4 engines to Northeast. Visibility excellent - nothing in sight. The Commanding Officer commends the officers and crew of the GROWLER for their conduct, actions and attention to duty during this attack and afterwards. All were in the keeping with the highest traditions of the U.S. Naval service.

"The patrol reports don't tell all of the details of the runs we made, nor what really happened. Actually the boat was not trimmed. We dove and hit an undersea mountain peak. That tore off both sound heads and messed up the outer doors on ballast tanks at about six-hundred feet. Duke Jordan and I blew numbers one and two main ballast tanks, or partially, from the after room and that's what put the sharp angle on the boat. Art Ullrich always had his battle station in the maneuvering room. Twice he had backed down in an emergency to pull us out of steep dives. He did this without orders from control. This was one of those instances when quick action may have saved the boat."

Schade recalled that *Growler*'s crew was hailed as "a bunch of unruly heroes," and what they had been drinking was actually a local form of white lightning called "Okuina." Executive officers had the additional responsibility of a ship's crew while on shore leave. That was also true on board, so as to give the skipper full concentration on his duties of finding the enemy and destroying it.

In his endorsement of *Growler*'s first run, Adm. R.M. English applauded Skipper Gilmore and his crew for a very successful war patrol. Aside from several casualties to a torpedo tube, an auxiliary engine, switch gears, sound head, periscope, stern plane and propeller shafts, *Growler* was able to operate reasonably well. There were various minor illnesses, but none were incapacitating. The ship was kept comfortably warm except when running silently. Heaters were secured then and the ship would become cold and clammy.

There were certain lessons learned by *Growler*'s first patrol. In that bleak part of the world, the Aleutians presented a problem of visibility. So running on the surface at slow speeds in low visibility broadened the horizon even though range of visibility was no better by eye or binoculars than by periscope. And, secondly, not too much reliance could be placed on sound gear.

When submerged, visibility increased to three or four miles when clear of land. The Aleutians are a barren chain of islands extending nine hundred miles west of Alaska. They are known to be fog-bound for most of the year. They are in the same latitude as Great Britain, which also suffers from lots of fog.

The strategies used by *Growler* to minimize the problem of visibility were satisfactory as long as the presence of the submarine was unknown. The trouble with that is that was never the case as the reports show. After the successful Independence Day attack on destroyer row, *Growler* was never able to close Kiska Harbor again, being forced out of the One Hundred Fathom Bank on each attempt.

On 7 July, when the heavy cruiser was sighted, *Growler* attempted to close by periscope and lost the vessel in the fog. Periscope search was made for almost two hours followed by a surface search. Additionally, the enemy vessel was never heard by sound. Finally, when *Growler* contact was reconnected, it was in the worst possible attack position.

The following was the opinion of *Growler*'s skipper, Gilmore:

"If enemy combatant vessels are present, or suspected of being present, in all cases of visibility, submerge and run silent while listening. Accept less broad horizon.

"If enemy vessels are not antisubmarine (a/s) vessels, they will immediately make radical zigs on detecting any submarine. Hence, submerged running should:

"A. Enhance chances of attack because submarine will not be sighted.

"B. Certainly decrease detection and increase close of ship.

"If enemy vessels are a/s, submarine has better chance of avoiding an attack or of pressing home own attack if submerged. It is realized that much dependence is placed on sound gear. Case in point is that on 6 July when *Growler* was submerged within 1,000 yards of that vessel which was avoided. On 7 July, the destroyer was never heard. Apparently, it never heard *Growler*, either surfaced or submerged, prior to sighting. In the latter case it is believed that had the *Growler* been submerged, the destroyer would probably not have detected her and *Growler* might have been able to press the attack."

Skipper Gilmore concluded that on returning to the area of the sighting of the cruiser, a grave mistake had been made by not submerging immediately even though the enemy was lost on the previous occasion; submerged search at least gave the submarine some measure of protection. "When the presence of combatant type... is as well established, as was it in this case, it is my opinion that I risked *Growler* unnecessarily by surface running in low visibility."

According to reports, miles covered while on station: 210 submerged for ninety-three hours; 555 on surface for eight-five hours. The total distance steamed on *Growler's* first war patrol was 6,140 miles. Total consumption of fuel 44,925 gallons.

July 1943. Above, from right: Lt. John Cunningham, Comdr. Howard Gilmore, Lt. Comdr. Arnold Schade, Lt. Landon Davis. Others unidentified. Below: The Growler *crew poses at Dutch Harbor after sinking three Japanese destroyers.*

Among other comments, Admiral English noted in his endorsement was that *Growler* subjected torpedoes to excessive pressure by going to deep submergence with the torpedo tube muzzle doors open. Submarines must insure that torpedo tube outer doors are closed when going deep to prevent flooding of torpedo afterbodies and emploders and possible damage resulting from depth charge attack. Submarine torpedo afterbodies may not be expected to withstand excessive pressures.

High Anxiety!

During the Battle for Guadalcanal, when the Marines landed on 7 August, *Growler* had already departed on its second and most successful war patrol to the East China Sea on 5 August 1942. It lasted forty-nine days and resulted in the sinking of four ships—a total of 26,000 tons.

5 August 1942.
> 0700   Departed Pearl Harbor enroute Midway under escort. Conducted daily dives and drills.

9 August 1942.
> 0811   Moored at Midway, fueled; U.S.S. Fulton repaired JK-QC sound gear.

10 August 1942.
> 0717   Under way for patrol station. Conducted daily drills enroute.

Entering her area northwest of Formosa (Taiwan) on the 21st, *Growler* conducted submerged night patrols. She continued to stand toward Taiwan, and on the 23rd she submerged thirty miles east of Taiwan near Kasho To maintaining high periscope patrol.

After dark *Growler* sighted and attacked a freighter by firing two torpedoes. Both torpedoes ran under their target and failed to explode. She surfaced to give chase. Visibility was excellent due to a full moon but the target was hazy against a land background. The freighter's quick exit into shallow waters prevented *Growler* from a deck gun attack. There was also the danger of enemy shore batteries. *Growler* submerged and changed course south toward Takao southwest of Taiwan.

Schade recalled that in the early morning of the 25th, patrolling amidst a large fishing fleet of one hundred to one hundred-fifty boats, *Growler* sighted and fired three torpedoes at a large passenger freighter. All three torpedoes missed. A three-hour depth-charge attack ensued, in which some fifty-three ash cans were dropped, causing extreme anxiety. One man who had been at the bow plane station during the attack and counterattacks became hysterical. He was given a morphine hypodermic and in three days returned to normal. He resumed watches after six days.

Growler surfaced and almost, immediately spotted a convoy. After two hours of maneuvering, she failed to come up to the main body of the convoy but did fire and sink the powerful gunboat *Senyo Maru.*

No more ships appeared in this immediate area for three days, which gave all hands a needed rest. *Growler* shifted to the east side of the island in the Pescadores channel. Then on the night of the 30th, while on the surface she sighted a large steamer at a range of 4,000 yards and swung 150 to the west at high speed to close. Three torpedoes were fired at an estimated range of 1,200 yards. Target spotted *Growler* and started swinging away fast, before the last torpedo was fired, successfully maneuvering to avoid being hit. The enemy was manning deck guns so *Growler* submerged as the enemy commenced firing.

Reports said that in the early morning of the 31st, a ship was sighted at, a range of five miles. *Growler* closed to 5,000 yards and due to the bright moonlight submerged for approach. Fired two torpedoes at a range of 1,000 yards. Both hit the *Elfuku Maru*, a 5,866-ton cargo ship that broke in two and sank in ninety seconds. *Growler* had sighted her and sunk her within forty minutes.

On 4 September *Growler* sighted a darkened sampan trailing her in the early morning which she sank by expending six rounds from her 3 ½-inch deck gun. At dawn *Growler* sighted masts of a large ship zigzagging at a distance of twelve miles. She closed on surface and when within range, submerged for the attack. The ship zagged across *Growler*'s stern at, a range of 1,800 yards. At 1,000 yards, she fired two torpedoes. Both hit at the bridge and forward. Enemy tanker took angle down by bow—screws clear of water and the crew manned abandoned ship stations. As after torpedoes, expended *Growler* swung about for bow shot. The tanker was yawing considerably. *Growler* fired another torpedo which missed. Then at 700 yards another was fired which hit and sank the *Kashino Maru*, a 4,000-ton supply ship, in two minutes.

A few days later, on the 8th, *Growler* established a submerged patrol on line south of Menka Sho. A destroyer patrolling the area remained in *Growler*'s area all day. As it never spotted her, Gilmore believed that it was probable that the Japanese were throwing all of their patrols in that area. So he decided to take *Growler* back to Takao and the Pescadores.

On the 13th, while patrolling north of Puki Kaku, *Growler* sighted a scattered convoy consisting of seven freighters and one destroyer at a distance of eight to twelve miles. She made an approach so as to get in on the fifth ship which was about three miles astern of the destroyer. She was the largest ship in the convoy, which was basically in two sections. *Growler* obtained a position ahead of the target and then diverged on an opposite course until 1,000 yards from track. The target was not zigging but was screened by two patrol boats.

Growler fired four torpedoes at an estimated range of 850 yards with a divergent spread. Although there were two explosions, Gilmore believed they all missed. When observed three minutes later the enemy ship appeared to be undamaged. After firing, patrol boats came toward firing point. *Growler* ran astern of the target and then between two after ships in the convoy, evading patrol boats at periscope depth. Sound conditions in the area north of Puki Kaku were extremely poor which helped *Growler* to escape.

18 September 1942:

    1000   Sighted vessel bearing 192° true, Northerly course, range 15 miles. Closed on surface to 6,000 yards. Identified as hospital ship "HIKAWA MARU" It was properly marked. Proceeded enroute (CONTACT #37).

Growler concluded one of the summer's best patrols by sending to the bottom more than 26,000 tons of the enemy's ships. On 15 September *Growler* cleared patrol area and arrived back in Pearl Harbor on 30 September.

During the Battle of Midway in early June, a young Tennessee native was on his first ship assignment. Leonard D. Greenwood, who had joined the Navy in February of 1942, was on the submarine tender, USS *Fulton* (AS-11) in Pearl Harbor and was assigned to a submarine relief crew that performed repair work on any submarine alongside.

Greenwood had completed electrical school and was a striker for petty officer 3rd class electricians mate.

After the Battle of Midway, the *Fulton* was sent to Midway to set up a submarine base. Greenwood recalls that the *Fulton* dropped anchor in a lagoon just inside the reef and started the development of the base. The Japanese left two buildings untouched: Gooney Bird Hotel (the TransWorld Airline rest stop before the war), and a ten- or twelve-unit development in various stages of construction from foundation to almost-completed multi-storied houses. Greenwood speculates that the enemy intended to use these buildings as housing when they took the island.

Greenwood's first duty at Midway was as a part of a daily working party put ashore to complete construction of the houses. This type of work was later to become the function of Sea Bees or CBs (construction battalions). Midway became a very efficient submarine base.

After some months during the establishment of the base and working in submarine repair, Greenwood requested the chief to put him on the first submarine in need of a electrician striker. A few days later *Growler*, just finishing her second war patrol after forty-nine days to the East China Sea, arrived at Midway.

Growler, coming alongside *Fulton*, backed into the reef and became hung on it at low tide. Two patrol torpedo (PT) boats raced around *Growler* to create wakes to shake her loose. Those efforts were unsuccessful and the *Growler* was freed only when the tide came in some hours later. Divers, inspecting the underside, discovered a bent screw, which meant that *Growler* had to go to the nearest dry-dock in Pearl Harbor to replace the screw and undergo a refit.

Greenwood got his wish: He was transferred to *Growler* and returned with her to Pearl Harbor. Life on the submarine was a new experience for him. The chief of the boat (COB) told him to drop his seabag down the crews' mess hatch and stow it anywhere he could in the crews' quarters until later. First impressions are usually vivid, and in Greenwood's case there was no difference. It was difficult because he was new among a crew that had already experienced two war patrols. He had no assigned bunk or locker but he did locate a small drawer to stow his toilet articles. After being on a relatively large ship, adjusting to the cramped quarters of a submarine was not an easy transition. And, he had to adjust to his new environment quickly. His major adjustment was "hot bunking," which meant sharing the same bunk with someone else who was not especially keen on the idea of sharing his space.

The life of a submariner had its ups and downs, and while very stressful, there were lighter moments. Once they were back in Hawaii, life in the Royal Hawaiian was not so grim. Greenwood may have even participated in sterno/turpentine parties, which would have required Executive Officer Schade to have to answer to Admiral Nimitz again.

In any event, there were better experiences during this period of the war. And it is likely along with recollections of the battles and life at sea, sailors will remember the popular songs of that year were: "Sleepy Lagoon," "Praise the Lord and Pass the Ammunition," and "That Old Black Magic."

Greenwood especially enjoyed the richly deserved luxury of the "rest and recreation" (R&R) respites at the Royal Hawaiian. It gave him and the other crew members the space to stretch and move about after days in cramped quarters.

Adm. R. H. English, commander of the Submarine Force, Pacific Fleet, gave *Growler* high marks for her second patrol. He said in his endorsement that "the area assigned was covered thoroughly, all attacks were aggressively prosecuted, and results obtained were satisfying."

On the second attack, the follow-up for an additional shot at a large transport, already damaged by the initial torpedo hit and observed to be down by the head with her screw out of the water, was admirably done. Though antisubmarine escorts were headed for the *Growler*, she fired one additional torpedo which hit. The commanding officer remained at periscope depth, and delivered the *coup de grace* with a second attack, thereby insuring the sinking of the transport. The commanding officer, officers, and crew of the *Growler* were to be congratulated for a second very successful patrol. The *Growler* was credited with the sinking of five enemy vessels for a total of 25,946 tons, according to reports and English's endorsement.

During its forty-nine day patrol, *Growler* had traveled 4,370 miles from Pearl Harbor via Midway to its patrol area off Taiwan. On station she patrolled 641 miles submerged and on surface 2,840 miles for a total of 3,481 miles. Then *Growler* covered 4,355 miles back to Pearl Harbor. In all, *Growler* had gone a total of 12,206 miles on her second war patrol and consumed 87,977 gallons of fuel oil. Expenditure of torpedoes was the cause of ending the patrol.

It was a patrol of high anxiety but it reminded Schade of the things that happened during these periods. He recalls that in one incident, a crewman disappeared for two days. Now how does someone go AWOL on a submarine? It happened, says Schade. During a depth-charge attack the lost soul had crawled into a torpedo tube. After the depth-charge attack, he had fallen asleep, emerging over twenty-four hours later.

Then there was suicide. One crewman was so terrified that he went into the battery area and died. He left a note that he didn't want to bring dishonor onto the boat and had decided to end his life.

The Japanese Naval Research Station in Yokosuka developed two sizes of depth charges—132 and 550 pounds—from conventional bombs, but their fuses were primitive as they were controlled by timers rather than by water pressure. The maximum setting of sixteen seconds caused the charge to go off at 250 feet, which had been more effective than they had been set for earlier in the war. American subs could easily dive much deeper and be out of the most effective part of the explosion.

"It was then that a dark cloud appeared which caused ten American submarines to be lost—about eight hundred lives. One of the most stupid legislators ever to darken the halls of the United States House of Representatives, Congressman Andrew Jackson May gave aid and comfort to the enemy after a tour of the front. He announced at a press conference that American submarines were doing just fine because the Japanese set their depth charges to explode too soon," according a story in the *Kangaroo Express*.

"COMSUBPAC Commander Lockwood was beside himself with rage, calculating that this leak caused submarines and their crews to be lost!

"But this was not the only innocent slip of the tongue committed by a big mouth. In June of 1942, Col. Robert R. McCormick of the *Chicago Tribune* and associated publications, announced that Americans had broken the Japanese secret code and were reading their messages before the battles of the Coral Sea and Midway!

"This time, though, the Japanese could not believe that anyone was able to read their complicated code and never acted on that information.

"The depth-charge tip was unfortunately acted upon. That led to the submarine service to be known as the "Silent Service" when all reporters were barred from subs.

"During the war when a sub was lost there would appear a short notice, 'The USS *Growler* is overdue and presumed lost.' After the war the accomplishments of subs were finally made public, but by that time the world was sick of war and general interest was not there. The name Silent Service remained and the 25 percent loss of personnel became lost in the history books."

Truk Stop

The Truk Islands form a large island group in the Western Pacific 2,100 miles southeast of Tokyo and 900 miles northwest of Rabaul, New Guinea. The Truk Islands are part of the Eastern Carolines. Germany had bought the islands from Spain in 1899, but then lost them to Japan as a mandate after World War I. It became a great Japanese naval base used by Japan in World War II as a stopping off point for shipping of reinforcements and war supplies from Japan to Rabaul, New Britain during World War II. Truk was the Japanese equivalent of the United States Pearl Harbor.

Growler had arrived at Pearl Harbor 30 September 1942 from her second war patrol. She commenced refit 1 October 1942, by submarine base personnel and was docked for propeller replacement by Navy yard forces, so that SJ radar and a 20 mm gun could be installed. Readiness for sea was 21 October 1942. One day was devoted to training on 20 October 1942.

At 0900 on 22 October, *Growler* departed Pearl Harbor in company with USS *Tarpon* under escort. At 1945 *Tarpon* departed and *Growler* diverged on a course to southward.

Growler was directed to Truk where she joined other United States submarines—*Drum, Tarpon, Pollack, Plunger, Grayling, Stingray* and *Silversides*—in the blockade of Truk, stopping the Japanese supplies.

Skipper Gilmore stated in his report for on 2 November 1942: "Entered area at eastern edge. Continued on surface until 1230 when Tanga Island was distant twenty miles, submerged, adjusted SJ radar at night using island peaks." From information available and estimate of probable Japanese movements, Gilmore decided to cover the east cape to Truk route as the most probable track. Patrolling at the southern edge of the area would best cover all probable lanes through this area from Shortlands, Buka and Rabaul to Truk.

Growler maintained her patrol in the area until mid-November. It reconnoitered at the east coast of New Ireland and western cove of Tanga island. Lights were observed on latter of 11 November. From the number of lights, Gilmore believed the Japanese might be engaged in construction work on the island. However, inspection of cove and shores from range of 3,000 yards disclosed nothing. Gilmore held daily drills in ship and fire control, according to Greenwood.

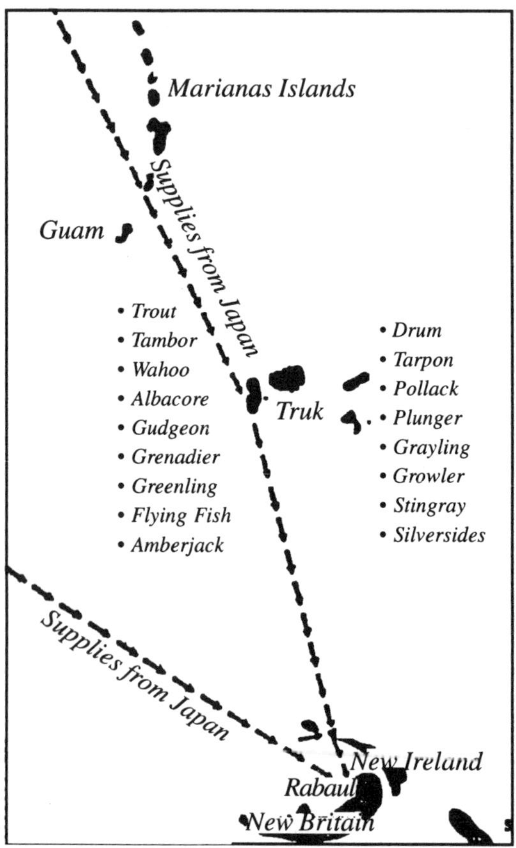

Sketch map showing approximate positions of the submarines, including Growler, *in the blockade of Truk.*

Growler's crew was divided into three watch sections—four hours on and eight off. Greenwood's watch was in the control room which controlled diving and surfacing. In general, submarines at the start of World War II remained submerged during the day to avoid detection, surfacing at night to recharge the boat's batteries. Greenwood's station was on the bow and stern planes, within six feet of the cob chief electrician on the hydraulic manifold. The chief constantly instructed Greenwood concerning everything in the control room and below in the pump room. Greenwood was grateful to the chief for making sure that he became "a proper submariner." The chief encouraged Greenwood to become worthy of his "dolphins" (the insignia designating submariners). But he had to study, study, study when not on watch. Making mistakes are, and were then, an unavoidable way of learning, according to Greenwood.

Life aboard the *Growler* did not compare favorably with the Royal Hawaiian. There were drills and there were more drills. There were drills for battle stations—whether on surface or submerged; fire drills, collision drills, and on and on until every contingency was met by an automatic reaction. Captain Gilmore never chewed anyone out, but one knew when there was a mistake, according to Greenwood. Officers, however, were excepted. In one instance, when the diving officer did not compensate for fuel consumption by adding an adequate amount of sea water to maintain proper trim, got a well deserved "ass chewing."

The whole point of all of the drills and proper knowledge of each other's job was that everyone depended on everyone to know their job and to properly perform their job. A weak link could cause the loss of everyone on board. Submariners were volunteers, hence, a very close group.

From Gilmore's records:

17 November 1942:

0140	Rec'd Message Nr 55 re Marus arriving at point 430 miles west of northwest corner of GROWLER area.
0205	Underway at two engine speed to intercept Marus.
1730	Slowed to one engine speed due to heavy head seas.

19 November 1942:

0320	Arrived at estimated point of intercept. Visibility poor. Seas too heavy for efficient high periscope patrol submerged. Remained on surface.
1717	Received Message Nr 56. Apparently there has been a change in area limits which GROWLER did not receive. Definitely this vessel is not in proper position for interception of Marus. Checked every message rec'd. All SUB's 42 messages nr 13 to 58 inclusive on hand and fully decoded. Proceeded eastward toward original area since GROWLER is not in position desired by Task Group Commander.
2205	Sent GROWLER message nr. 2 giving information as to position and movement in hopes of clarifying situation as to areas.

Growler's new patrol area in the Solomon islands across the key Truk-Rabaul shipping lanes in these days of bitter fighting over Guadalcanal was to block enemy shipping.

Greenwood's typical day running submerged was, depending upon the assigned patrol area, the weather and luck, with no targets, very boring:

0355	Relieved watch in maneuvering room, making ten knots on two main engines.
0530	Moved to within five miles from mouth of enemy harbor.
0610	Sighted enemy patrol boat and dawn patrol plane. Periscope search every twenty minutes—sound gear reports enemy screws weaker.
0700	Breakfast for those going on watch. Made log entries.
0750	Relieved from watch, making sixty turns on battery and headed for breakfast. Watered storage batteries. Rested for six hours with some sleep.
1450	Up early—brushed teeth—washed face—headed for mess.
1600	On watch running submerged ten miles from land.
1710	Sound gear reports two explosions long way off. Periscope watch reports nothing but two small fishing boats headed to port.
1845	Rigged for red (only red lights in conning tower and control room to enhance night vision topside).
1905	Surfaced—two main engines on propulsion and one on battery charge—all ahead standard—made log entries.
2000	Relieved from watch—propulsion the same—continuing battery charge—coffee and snack in crews mess listened to short wave radio news from San Francisco—war drags on.

In combat action everything was different—nothing was typical.

20 November 1942:

0343	Rec'd message nr 57 giving new area assignments.
1920	Sent msg nr 3 regarding non receipt (previous to msg nr 57) of change of area and requesting clarification. Realized Japs would probably D/F this vessel, but believed msg nr 3 was justified because, if GROWLER was at fault in its communications, doubt and confusion might arise with the result that this vessel might be in the same area as another US submarine with possible fatal consequences.
2220	Rec'd msg nr 58 regarding Jap submarines and destroyers enroute to Rabaul. Following times of transit for enemy vessels through GROWLER area were estimated: Destroyers - 0400 to 2400, 22 November. S/M's first group - 1600 or later, 22 November. S/M's second group - 1200 or later, 23 November. Plan to cover Truk-Kavieng and Truk Steffen Strait routes, remaining north of 100 fathom curve as southern boundary. Deemed it inadvisable to cross 100 fathom curve because: (a) Japanese may have mined part of shallow water. (b) Charts available are not very good. (c) That area is probably under most intensive air and surface patrol.

29–30 November 1942:
> Since all vessels evaded us, decided to patrol at upper limits
> of area. Enemy vessels had succeeded in evasion by radi-
> cal zigs either east or west after clearing shallow areas.
> Estimated chances of interception would be better by pa-
> trolling at northern limits, playing them to pass Tench
> Island to eastward.

4 December 1942:
> Proceeded on surface along northern edge of area
> and then down neutral lane at 154 long, enroute Brisbane.

In late 1942 a new commander, Rear Adm. James Fife, replaced Admiral Christie as commander of Task Force Forty-two, headquartered in Brisbane, Australia. Fife believed the generally poor showing of United States submarines basing in Brisbane up to then was due to over-caution. When he assumed command of the task force, he abandoned caution. Each of his skippers would give a good accounting of himself or else he would be summarily relieved.

Admiral Fife was firm but fair. His strategy was to get the war over with and a way to do that was to be aggressive. Many great leaders accused of being reckless while in the short run incurring high casualties, probably had lower casualties in the long run by being aggressive. So it seems to be the case with Admiral Fife. There has been a comparison of Fife to German Adm. Karl Doenitz in that Fife employed the "wolf pack" concept in his submarine deployments against the Japanese.

Admiral Fife urged his submarine commanders to "press home all attacks." His standing orders were "pursue relentlessly," remembering that the mission is to destroy every possible enemy ship. "Do not allow cripples to escape or leave them to sink—make sure that they do sink," were his words.

Until then most skippers had been assigned an area to patrol and were left pretty much on their own. Before the Japanese changed their codes in February, there had been a steady flow of information from the codebreakers about Japanese Maritime Forces reinforcing the Solomon Islands from Palau and Truk. Fife believed the submarine force could better capitalize on this information if the boats were more tightly controlled from Brisbane, and shifted about frequently as targets became known. He believed he should take a direct and firm hand in the shifting or, as he told his staff, he was "playing checkers" with submarines.

In the end, between 1943 and 1945, the Pacific Submarine Force sank more than 1,000 enemy ships, amounting to six million tons and damaged at least 500 more. This fact was a major cause of Japan's defeat. The cost to the United States was a loss of 52 out of a total of 314 submarines and a loss of 3,500 men who went down with the boats. It does not include those killed in action, such as Gilmore. The submarine force was a major cause of Japan's defeat and Commander Schade played no small part in the defeat of the Japanese Navy.

Take Her Down!

On 1 January 1993, just as the battle for Guadalcanal was winding down, *Growler* departed Brisbane, Queensland under escort of USS *Mugford* on her fourth war patrol on 1 January 1943 which was to prove to be one of the most gallant actions in naval history. She arrived on 10 January in her assigned area off the coast of New Britain, New Ireland and New Hanover Islands, covering the approaches to Rabaul and Kavieng to harry the enemy's traffic lanes between Rabaul and the western Solomons.

No sooner had she reached the area than her periscope was up to its neck in torpedo attacks. The area was patrolled continuously by air and all sea vessels were escorted by antisubmarine ships. Fife, manning his radio nightly, chivvied *Growler* around, trying to put Gilmore in the path of known convoys or other targets, according to Hagendorn.

On the night of 15 January, *Growler* was scouting six miles northwest of Waton Island and on the following morning, she got a big one: the 6,000-ton passenger-cargo ship *Chifuku Maru.* She had sighted a convoy at a distance of ten miles. As it was later determined, the convoy consisted of eight Marus escorted by two patrol boats and one *Asashio*-class destroyer. The convoy was in two loose columns about five hundred yards apart with one patrol boat to the north and one patrol boat to the south.

Gilmore then moved *Growler* to approach so as to fire at the northern column. She got inside of northern patrol boat and was in a flood firing position on northern column at 2,000-yards range when the whole convoy zigzagged at *Growler,* giving Gilmore no other alternative than to fire at the southern column. Gilmore planned to swing and try to get bow shots in at after ships.

The reports of 16 January read:

1005	Fired two torpedoes at leading ship southern column, range 800 yards, 100° port track, speed 10 knots.....both torpedoes hit. Ship took heavy list to port and trimmed down heavily by the stern. Ship similar to BRISBANE MARU type, page 100. At the time GROWLER was in unfortunate predicament of being 400 yards from the DD. Swung hard toward formation and DD and had to go deep.
1007	DD dropped three depth charges which appeared to be no closer than 100–200 yards on starboard side. GROWLER cut back through formation which was evidently scattering.

After surviving more depth charge attacks and bombings by planes, *Growler* eluded the enemy. She went north submerged, surfacing at night in bright moonlight, continuing on assigned Rabaul tracks at the western edge of area. It was apparent that the enemy was searching the whole area for *Growler*.

For the next week *Growler* patrolled the Cape Lambert Light area off the New Ireland coast. There were reports that there were numerous enemy ships in the area. During this time the battle for Guadalcanal was winding down in favor of the American Marine and Army forces. Japan was desperately evacuating their army from the island. Although there were numerous enemy sightings during this time, *Growler* was not able to close in on any of them.

Growler was ordered north to patrol the New Hanover area. On 29 January she intercepted a Japanese convoy while patrolling on the surface. Submerging, *Growler* maneuvered into position for an attack on a freighter, the *Miyadono Maru*, a passenger-cargo carrier. Gilmore decided to patrol off coast of New Ireland. After receiving a message of a 4,000-ton ship with a submarine chaser escort *Growler* changed course to head for Cape Watui in hopes of intercepting the *Maru* there at daybreak. She then headed westward toward New Hanover to waylay traffic from Truk and Palau. On 30 January, *Growler* attacked and damaged a freighter. During this action she was driven deep by a tempest of gunfire and depth charges. On the last day of the month, she attacked a 2,500-ton converted gunboat with a single torpedo that ran under the target without exploding.

A few nights later, Fife put Gilmore on the trail of a small convoy, but escorts and mechanical failures on *Growler* prevented an attack. *Growler* later successfully penetrated a heavy screen and sank a 5,425-ton freighter by torpedo fire, both torpedoes fired scoring hits. On the 30th of January, a second freighter of about 6,500 tons was damaged by torpedo fire—further attacks were frustrated by gunfire from the target. Following each of these attacks, *Growler* was severely depth-charged, but her commanding officer, Gilmore, ably maneuvered his ship to avoid serious damage.

On other occasions when enemy vessels were sighted, Lieutenant Commander Gilmore was most aggressive in his efforts to reach a firing position, but initial long ranges and large angles on the bow prevented additional successful attacks. On 5 February, a dangerous leak developed in the forward torpedo room following a series of depth-charge attacks by enemy warships, but flooding was controlled and depth control maintained as a result of the prodigious efforts of a well-trained and well-directed crew.

The area teemed with enemy shipping and aggressive patrol craft. At this date the Japanese were making a last desperate attempt to evacuate the remnants of their Guadalcanal garrison. To the storm center, the Imperial Navy was rushing every gun, bomb and depth charge it could muster. As *Growler* continued to contact enemy vessels on every hand, it was apparent to Skipper Gilmore, that the antisubmarine measures were boiling the water off the Bismarks. Patrols meant convoys in which *Growler* was deployed.

According to naval records, on the night of 4 February, south of Steffen Strait, Gilmore put *Growler* on the trail of a convoy which was headed for Gazelle Channel, probably en route to Rabaul. Two merchantmen were under escort of two patrol vessels. Estimating their speed and course, Gilmore sent his submarine on a fast run southward to get *Growler* ahead of the convoy's projected track. By about 0300 the next morning, Gilmore had accomplished a complete end-around.

Two ships were sighted. Poor visibility necessitated a surface attack and Gilmore made a difficult attack. *Growler* closed the target and the torpedoes were readied for firing when the lead ship suddenly opened fire at 5,000 yards. Gilmore ordered a quick dive when the enemy commenced depth charging. This lasted for about an hour.

At about 0400 in the morning, a concussion ruptured a manhole gasket in the forward main ballast tank. Water flooded into the forward torpedo room at a rate of about 1,000 gallons an hour. Emergency repairs curbed the flood, but the damage was critical and could only be properly repaired on the surface.

Around 0530 the enemy was gone and Gilmore came up to periscope depth to survey the scene. A smokestack was seen about five miles away and was followed by a convoy. The torpedo room bilges were being held at a reasonable level by a drain pump, and the damage control party had managed to cover the leaking manhole with sheet rubber and deck plates held in place by shores and jacks. The flooding had been stopped but the leakage remained a threat. Under threat of another depth charge, Gilmore chose to evade the enemy for the present. With repairs of the ruptured manhole, *Growler* surfaced at midnight to search out the enemy once more.

From Skipper Gilmore's record:

6 February 1943:

    Submerged 8 miles north of WATON ISLAND, searched to east and west of WATON 2 miles from shore. No activity, no ships or patrol boats sighted.

2200   Sent radio message to Commander Task Force 42 as directed and proceeded to new area, speed 17 knots.

Growler was patrolling on the surface during the early hours of 7 February, when, at 0110, an enemy vessel (the *Hayasaki)* was sighted close aboard. According to George Wade, "compared to the *Growler,* the Jap ship was a giant tower, a 2,500 ton fighting man-o-war, made specially to combat subs. With the proverbial 'bone in her teeth,' she was bent on total destruction of the sub, on that fateful night. It all started with a high speed chase, rapid commands from the bridge, then a hard left rudder followed by the wail of the collision alarm."

7 February 1943

0110   Sighted ship on starboard bow opposite course, range 2000 yards. Contact # 46. Turned away, made tubes ready and swung around to close for attack....ship sighted us and reversed course to attack.

0134   Range too close on TDC and by radar to fire. Bridge gave order "Cap left full rudder" and sounded the collision alarm.

0135   GROWLER hit enemy vessel head on, swinging with left rudder, at 17 knots, striking him halfway between his bow and bridge. The impact was terrific, knocking everyone down; GROWLER heeled over about 50°. The enemy opened fire with several machine guns (.50 cal.) at point blank range. The order was given "Clear the bridge." The O.O.D. and quartermaster descended followed by two wounded survivors who were pulled through the Conning Tower hatch. About 30 seconds elapsed. No one else appeared at the hatch. Sounded diving alarm, close the hatch. Submerged.

The Commanding Officer, Assistant O.O.D. and one lookout were left on the bridge. It is believed they were killed by enemy gun fire and washed overboard. The enemy continued spraying the bridge with machine gun fire until it was under water.

0201   Made battle surface. Nothing in sight so cleared the area to westward....Lieutenant Commander A.F. SCHADE assumed command.

According to the February 1993 issue of the *Kangaroo Express*: "At the start of the battle *Growler* had turned away to prepare tubes for firing, then closing for attack. The night was dark and visibility very poor, but when the range was reduced to about 2,000 yards, *Hayasaki* sighted *Growler*, and changed course to ram. No longer in a position to fire, Commander Gilmore skillfully handled his ship to avoid the ramming attack of the enemy vessel, and having done so, then courageously and daringly turned the tables on the enemy.

"Below, anxious and alerted men, their taut nerves straining to the breaking point, knew something was going to happen and happen fast. The ship heeled to the command left full rudder, then almost simultaneously the collision and the diving alarms sounded. The *Growler* was fighting for her very life. The tremendous crash left the *Growler* rolling to 45 degrees and at the same time the thunderous roar of gunfire terrorized the crew as it penetrated the compartments. The ramming had sent everyone sprawling but bodily harm went unnoticed as the engine men desperately began rigging the room to dive by shutting down the diesels and closing the vents. Experienced hands worked frantically to complete the task. The *Growler* had been making seventeen knots, when she struck the enemy frigate broadside, ripping her side plating wide open. The impact was so great that *Growler* heeled over like a rolling log and when she righted the enemy gunboat opened fire at point blank range," according to the *Kangaroo Express*.

"George Wade was there, right next to Gilmore on the bridge, when all this was happening. A large caliber machine gun bullet hit George in his right hand, another hit John Baxley in his leg, but those wounds probably saved their lives as their limp, bleeding bodies were passed down below the decks. Machine-gun bullets still raked the hull of the *Growler* from stem to stern and it seemed as if the boat was in its final moments of life.

"On *Growler*'s bridge were Skipper Gilmore, the officer of the deck, the assistant OOD, the quartermaster, and three lookouts. Machine-gun fire from the enemy gunboat tore into Gilmore, Ensign W.W. Williams, Assistant Officer of the Deck and Fireman Wilbert F. Kelley, mortally wounding them. Gilmore gave the command 'clear the deck.' The Officer of the Deck, Quartermaster William Wagner and two bleeding lookouts descended through the hatch. Schade came up to assist the wounded survivors below.

"When *Growler*'s Commanding Officer Gilmore gave the order to clear the bridge he was in a position near the hatch, where he could have reached the comparative safety of the conning tower, but Gilmore, without regard to his own safety, bravely ordered the remainder of the bridge force to precede him. Four men, two of whom were wounded, reached the conning tower, but the heavy fusillade of .60 caliber bullets ripped through the thin side plating and severely wounded the captain and two others: Ensign W. Wadsworth Williams and lookout fireman W.F. Kelley. As the captain fell to the deck, his dying words were a clear order, 'Take her down,' knowing he would be left on the bridge.

"Badly and painfully bruised by the fall during the collision from the conning tower hatch to the deck of the control room, second-in-command Schade hesitated thirty seconds—save the ship or save the captain? Gilmore's order was clear. It was Schade's duty to do what was best for *Growler* and her crew. Schade obeyed orders and a legendary submarine story was made. He gave orders to dive, leaving Howard Gilmore, along with Williams and Kelley topside. No one knows how long Gilmore lived in the water. The Japanese apparently made no effort to capture him or the others. He probably drifted away in the darkness. For sacrificing his life to save his ship, Gilmore was posthumously awarded the medal of honor, the nation's highest award for valor in battle. He was the first man of the submarine force to be so decorated."

Schade's Recollections

"We were closing in with anti-sub frigate and there was a call to battle stations. I was in the conning tower manning the torpedo data computer, getting ready for torpedo firing when all of a sudden I realized we were going at 17 knots headed straight for this guy and within another couple of minutes we would be too close to fire torpedoes so I called up to the bridge, 'Hey, we're too close. Slow down.' And at that point, Gilmore was up on the bridge and he sent diving officer below. I stayed in the conning tower but at this time we were inside torpedo range. If you don't have at least five hundred yards to fire a torpedo, you can't fire it. You blow yourself up. So I said, 'We're insides firing range for torpedoes, I'd better stop and do something.' About this time they opened fire on us and all hell broke loose. And bullets were flying all over the place. That's when Gilmore said, 'Take her down, Arnie,' and I said, 'OK. Clear the bridge.' So we cleared the bridge and got them all down there, except that by this time two of the lookouts had been badly wounded and covered with blood and we were trying to shovel them down through the hatch. The lieutenant of the afterpart was killed and so was Gilmore and they were up on the deck and were just blown over the side. Both of them. I went up myself. I stuck my head through the hatch and yelled. There was nobody there but the two sailors who were wounded and we were dragging them down. So, by this time we had already had the word to 'take her down.' And the quartermaster, at that signal, mans the diving alarm. I turned to him and said, 'Sound the diving alarm.' And that's when we went down and found out that we were in bad shape. We had holes all over the place. The conning tower which had the torpedo controls was just full of holes.

"The ship was just a total mess. Water was gushing in from all sides from the top down. Several of the compartments were flooding. We were pumping and doing all kinds of things to keep the boat from sinking. There was nothing we could do about the torpedoes that were hanging out of the tubes. That was something. Scared the hell out of us if you run a torpedo for five hundred yards when it has been fired, it activates the exploder. We had to go more than five hundred yards with these torpedoes hanging out there. Finally got a message through to MacArthur that we were in sad shape and needed cover. He said to stay on the surface and they would provide air cover until we got back to Brisbane.

"When we got back into port with the ship, its bow in shambles and everything disrupted and torn apart, Jimmy Fife, who was the squadron commander there in Brisbane said he wanted to see all the chiefs from the *Growler*. I think there were six of them. They went up to his cabin. He said, "I have only one question for you. Do you want to go to sea with Arnie Schade as your captain, or do you want to go to sea on another submarine?' And to a man, they all said, 'We're going to stick with him no matter what.'

"My sailors want to stay with me. I was really grateful. I knew them. I trusted them and they trusted me and we had a good working solution for every problem, and we made sure we understood it. It was traumatic when *Growler* did go down, but most of (these men) survived. They had been transferred off like I had."

Now under the command of Lieutenant Commander Schade, *Growler*'s well-organized crew kept her under control in the face of dangerous leaks caused by the enemy's gunfire, with water in the control room and the pump room half flooded, was leveled off, and Schade, after thirty minutes gave the order to "battle surface" to fight the enemy once again. Torpedoes were hanging out of the bow tubes. With bow planes and vital auxiliaries inoperative, Schade, himself dazed and bruised from a fall from the conning tower to the control room, had his hands full. The impact of the collision had bent eighteen feet of the *Growler*'s bow at right angles to the submarine, rendering her forward torpedo tubes useless. Saltwater poured through bullet holes in the conning tower and hatch. The hatch was repaired by a number of men including Everett Jordan, Dan Bialko, and Arthur Ullrich.

Schade gave battle orders to surface and sink the *Hayasaki*, but when the *Growler* came up, the seas were empty. Schade believed the ramming had sunk her. At dawn Schade gave orders to head for Brisbane some two thousand miles away, arriving there on the 17 February for extensive repairs.

Packwood's Recollections

On 1 December 1942, Edward A. Packwood boarded the ill-fated patrol as a motorman 2nd class. Here is his dramatic account of this episode: Packwood was at his battle station in the after engine room where all four engines were on line.

"The electrician said we were doing 21 knots. There were six of us aft and six forward. I was standing with my right arm hooked through the ladder near the engine room hatch so that I could get cool air coming through the engine air induction.

"At our speed, we could feel a full-port turn. Our phone talker asked control what was happening. The word was radar had lost contact with our target and we were circling back two miles, trying to pick up the target again. Five or six minutes after coming on our new course we felt a sharp port turn and a minute later we hit! Diving and collision alarms went off together. I heard machine gun fire and smelled gun smoke coming through the air induction.

"By then I was hanging in the ladder with my right arm, standing on the #4 engine. The boat had violently rolled over and when we righted, I looked forward and could see none standing in either engine room. They had all been thrown forward and then rolled into the port corner. I got untangled from the ladder with a pulled shoulder.

"We already had a down angle so I shut down aft and closed the outboard exhaust. Then I dropped the induction flapper, looked into forward engine room where the crew was just picking themselves up. With my collision station under control, I ran through and helped secure the forward engine room. I grabbed the damage-control bag from the forward engine and was in control in time to help the two wounded in the crew mess and radio room.

"I was happy to hear damage in the forward torpedo room showed no water and the control room watch were calm and going through a normal routine. But the bullet that went through the conning tower hatch was flooding the conning tower where the lower hatch was shut. When we reached one-hundred twenty feet, the trim pump was put on the pump room bilge to get the water out that was draining down from the conning tower.

"Everything happened so fast that the only thought at the time was to do everything possible to secure the boat. But ever since then, a number of questions have plagued me. There seems never to have been mention of the bullet holes in the conning hatch and the starboard side of the bridge. The fold-down seat where the skipper died was nothing but splinters. The angle arm frame was shot out of shape and there were many other holes in the side as well as several through the after scope and scope shear. Another question is why were we going 21 knots approaching an enemy target on the surface during a night so black and full of rain squalls?

"My watch oiler had gone up for lookout just before battle stations. His name was Kelley—he didn't come home with us."

Because of the extensive damage suffered, *Growler* had to proceed on the surface, which slowed the speed by 30 percent. A report was sent to Admiral Fife that *Growler* was proceeding via the emergency routing. Fife

Declassified U. S. Navy photograph

Lt. Comdr. Arnold Schade is awarded his second Silver Star and the Navy Cross by Vice Adm. Arthur S. Carpender after the completion of the fourth war patrol.

was in the same building as General MacArthur, who arranged air cover through the straights, which were heavily patrolled by the Japanese. She arrived at Brisbane on 17 February for extensive repairs.

Endorsing *Growler*'s fourth patrol report, Admiral Fife commended "the performance of the officers and crew in effecting repairs and bringing the ship safely back to base is one of the outstanding submarine feats of the war to date. *Growler* will be repaired and will fight again."

Admiral Halsey wrote: "The force commander is proud to extend his congratulations and commendation to this valiant ship and her courageous crew.

Leonard Greenwood's second war patrol, *Growler*'s fourth, turned out to be almost his last. This was one of the worst things that happened to him. The sound of .50 caliber machine gun bullets ripping into the *Growler* after ramming an enemy ship, resulting in the loss of his skipper, a gunnery officer, a lookout and two badly wounded lookouts, is something Greenwood said he will never forget. The difficulties of reaching port after the ramming put unbelievable stress on the entire crew and they did more than just their jobs.

Growler had spent ten days limping back to New Farm Wharf in Brisbane, Australia, pushing water up before her staved bow. The distance from Rabaul to Brisbane is about two-thousand miles and *Growler*'s speed could not exceed much more than eight knots an hour. Torpedoes were hanging from their tubes, which Schade said "scared the hell out of us." Back in port, the *Growler* was repaired in three months by the Australians who dubbed her the "Kangaroo Express." The Aussies were so proud of their new bow that they welded a metal kangaroo on each side of *Growler*'s bow.

Lieutenant Commander Schade succeeded Gilmore, and at the age of thirty-one became the Navy's youngest submarine commander. The *Growler* was returned to service, making it doubly historic, as perhaps the only United States submarine to purposely ram and sink an enemy ship in World War II, and possibly the most severely damaged warship to return to battle. Commander Schade was awarded his second Silver Star and the Navy Cross for the safe return of the *Growler* and its crew. Because Schade had been injured in the collision with the *Hayasaki*, he was also awarded the Purple Heart.

In addition to being the first submariner to earn the Congressional Medal of Honor, Skipper Gilmore was also awarded, posthumously, the Purple Heart, "For distinguished gallantry and valor above and beyond the call of

July 1943. Below, left, Leonard Greenwood and a friend on leave in Sydney, Australia after the fourth war patrol. Below, right, Lt. John Cunningham enjoys some shore food on leave in Brisbane, Australia.

Photo courtesy of Leonard Greenwood.

Photo courtesy of Leonard Greenwood.

duty...in the terrific fire of the sinking gunboat's heavy machine guns, Commander Gilmore, refusing safety for himself, remained on deck while his men preceded him below ....."

And those Purple Hearts mailed to the next of kin who were killed during that 7 February *Growler* engagement with *Hayasaki*, were for Ensign William W. Williams and Fireman 3rd Class Wilbert F. Kelley. The first living submariner to be presented a Purple Heart was Torpedoman 3rd Class John A. Baxley, one of the surviving *Growler* lookouts. He received his Purple Heart from the commanding officer of the Oak Knoll Naval Hospital on 6 July 1943. The other wounded *Growler* lookout who survived, Gunner's Mate 3rd Class George Wade, didn't get his Purple Heart until 29 September 1943, while recuperating at the U.S. Naval Hospital, Treasure Island. In the memory of the U.S. Submarine Force the names of Gilmore and *Growler* are welded—inseparable. Mention either, and submariners will think of gunfire and chaos in a roaring sea—a submarine's life threat-

Photo courtesy of Leonard Greenwood

Left, George Wade recovering from wounds received in the ramming of the Hayasaki. *Below, Lt. Landon "Big Stinky" Davis.*

Photo courtesy of Leonard Greenwood.

ened—and a voice speaking out of the night: "Take her down!"

At the time Harry Messick was on the *Fulton*. He said, "From 1942 to 1943 the *Fulton* established submarine bases at Midway Island and Brisbane, Australia. One of my collateral duties was as cable officer which involved trips to the local bank to cable money from the crews of the submarines, particularly on paydays, to United States destinations. Comdr. Howard W. Gilmore of the USS *Growler*, just before his final patrol run, had me cable his final payment of an insurance company loan. Was it a premonition or...?"

The Beginning of the End

"Imperial Japan and the United States had the same strategy to defeat their foes. Just as the idea of Hitler's *Blitzkrieg* was to knock out the enemy with a 'Lightning War,' both sides saw their victory in a quick final battle," said John Toland in the *Rising Sun.* "Admiral Isoroku Yamamoto reckoned that he had six months to a year in which to knock out the American Pacific Fleet. It was a race against time as the island nation depended upon foreign resources for its wartime supplies. Despite the American-led embargo just prior to the outbreak of war in the Pacific on crucial strategic raw materials such as oil, rubber and steel, Japan had ample stockpiles to wage war for about a year. So the *Blitzkrieg* was a crucial strategy for a decisive victory against her enemies.

"For both sides, the strategy was not effective for the next three years after Pearl Harbor—it was more of a war of attrition. Although the Allies won the Battle of Coral Sea off the coast of Australia, a month before the Battle of Midway on 4 to 6 June 1942, Midway ended Japan's expansion eastward and is widely considered the turning point of the naval war in the Pacific. However, many more sea battles were to be fought with major losses to both sides.

"If Midway was the turning point of the war at sea then Guadalcanal was the beginning of the end on the islands. In three thousand years, Japan had never lost a land war. The Japanese therefore had a feeling of invincibility, and their overconfidence would work against them. They underestimated the American will to fight.

"Allied strategy in the South Pacific had three major objectives: recapture the Philippines; cut Japan's lines of communications with its overseas bases, and set up bases from which to attack Japan—'Island Hopping.' But first the Allies had to capture or neutralize Rabaul, an important enemy base on New Britain island just north of Australia. They planned an invasion of the nearby Solomon Islands, while other Allied forces approached Rabaul by way of New Guinea.

"On 7 August 1942, the Allies began their first offensive action in the Pacific. U.S. Marines under Maj. Gen. Alexander A. Vandergrift landed on Guadalcanal in the Solomon Islands. The fighting was bitter and control of the island seesawed for several months.

"On 'Gadarukanaru' (Guadalcanal) Maj. Gen. Yumio Nasu, the Japanese commander of an infantry group had hastily moved into position for attacking the U.S. Marines, who were defending Henderson Air Field. After nightfall, the feeble Nasu, critically ill from malaria, led the first charge, using his sword as a cane. He managed to hobble across the line of barbed wire before a volley of rifle fire flashed in the dark. A bullet tore into Nasu's chest, severely wounding him.

"All along the line automatic weapons fire raked the attackers. Within minutes almost every man down to the company level was dead or wounded. Their men continued to drive forward. Whenever they were stopped, they reformed and charged again. The GIs and marines refused to give ground.

"In the lulls the two sides shouted at each other. 'Blood for the Emperor!' yelled a Japanese in English. 'Blood for Eleanor!' retorted a Marine. The shouting turned to insults. 'Tojo eat shit!' taunted a GI from the America division. There was a moment's pause, then from the other side: 'Babe Ruth eat shit!' according to Toland in *The Rising Sun.*

"The fighting continued until midnight," Toland wrote. "The assault was crushed and the survivors filtered back over the bodies of their comrades. In two days Nasu's attacks had left more than three thousand dead or dying in the uprooted jungle. It was if a fire storm had swept over the area. The wounded Nasu was carried on a litter back to division headquarters. As he held out a feeble hand to Lt. Gen. Masao Maruyama, his commander and friend, and opened his mouth to speak, he died."

By February 1943, Army troops under Maj. Gen. Alexander M. Patch finally cleared Guadalcanal, just about the time that skipper Schade on the crippled *Growler* was limping back to Brisbane passing through the Solomon Islands.

From 2 to 5 March 1943 the Allied forces of the United States, Britain and Holland defeated a Japanese naval force in the Battle of Bismarck Sea. While General MacArthur's land campaign was in full swing, Allied forces caught a major force of reinforcements bound for Lae, New Guinea. With Navy and Army Air Force attacks, the convoy was virtually destroyed.

Nose Job

Due to the extensive damage suffered by the collision with the *Hayasaki*, *Growler* had to proceed on the surface at a 30 percent loss of speed—eighteen feet of her bow had been bent at a right angle. She had to navigate through heavily patrolled enemy waters from above New Ireland down past the Solomon Islands where fierce battles were taking place on her return to Brisbane. Skipper Schade had sent a report to Admiral Fife that *Growler* was returning via emergency routing. When General MacArthur, who was above Fife's office in Brisbane, was advised of *Growler*'s plight, he ordered an air cover for her through the straits. *Growler* spent ten days limping back to new Farm Wharf about two thousand miles distant, pushing water up before her staved bow. Schade recollects that two armed torpedoes hanging from her bow "scared the hell out of us."

On this patrol, Greenwood had stood his watches "in the maneuvering room as the junior man on the controllers. Lieutenant Cunningham was the communications officer and every time that I spoke to him, my standard question was, "What's the dope." He always answered a few words that I considered a bit of news which was very much appreciated for scuttlebutt among crew members. This was the patrol on which the ramming took place when all hands worked their ass off in trying to make it back to port. After the ramming, only four of the six torpedoes could be pulled from the tubes, leaving the two hanging out of the bow. They were armed, and a great danger to *Growler*, other boats in port and the tender *Fulton*. This problem was soon solved, which is a great story in itself."

Before the war, William R. Davis had served on the S-45 until his transfer to *Growler* in early 1942. At the time, he was torpedo man 3rd class in the afternoon. Davis made *Growler*'s first three war patrols. During *Grower*'s fourth patrol, he had remained in Brisbane.

Because Gilmore was killed in action, Schade, as executive officer, was now responsible for bring *Growler* back to port. Davis recalls *Growler*'s return to Brisbane. "I met the boat as it was backing up into the bay. The torpedoes were still on the boat, so we removed all of them, except for the two sticking out of the tubes.

"The boat was anchored in the middle of the bay. Del Hilsabeck and I volunteered to remove the exploder mechanisms. We did it, Del and I. There was no one else aboard. Both torpedoes were fully armed.

"We were both confined to the boat while the old bow was cut off and replaced in dry-dock. We bore-sighted and aligned the tubes. We ground the lands in the tubes for days until the gage went through.

"I left the Growler 1st class. We then got two weeks leave and Mr. Joslins got the medal. No regrets. I'm still alive."

Davis was on board when *Growler* proceeded on her fifth war patrol on 13 May 1943 for the Solomon Islands.

Greenwood remembered "the happiness all around when the communications officer, Lieutenant Cunningham, announced that we are not leaving Brisbane to be repaired. There was a civilian dry-dock up river large enough to handle us, but the workers there had never been close to a submarine. The blueprints needed for our repair had to be flow in from Groton. It was necessary to set up the blocks on which the *Growler* would rest during her dry-dock stay.

"After those two dangerous torpedoes were disarmed and removed by "Stinky" Davis and Del Hilsabeck, *Growler* was tied up at New Farm Wharf up river from the Fulton, awaiting further movement to its dry-dock.

"Lieutenant Cunningham had either purchased or leased a British automobile that burned real hard-to-get petrol. How did he did this is unknown to me," said Greenwood, but he had the connections and funds. "The day we were to move to dry-dock, and just before the lines were cast off, he looked at me and handed me a set of keys to the car and stated that I had permission to leave the boat and drive his car to the dry-dock parking lot.

"As I got to the gangway, which was ready to be pulled, the gangway watch asked me where the hell I thought I was going. I replied, 'Ashore, man, ashore.' I found the car okay and watched *Growler* move up river.

"Anyone who could drive knew how to operate a clutch and shift gears. What surprised me was that the steering was on the right side and the gears were completely backwards. Needless to say, I had to practice up and down New Farm parking area using back streets where there was no traffic.

"I had no idea where the dry-dock was in relation to where I was, except it was up the river. So I practiced my driving on every street that dead-ended at the river front. More than an hour passed before I found the area for the dry-dock people located near a laundry and an inviting pub. Of course I walked across the street to the pub to get directions and a beer. I arrived just in time to enter the gate and witness *Growler* being safely and carefully pushed into the dry-dock.

"A week or two later, the squadron commander pitched a big beer party for the entire crew. At about 0200 in the morning, as we entered the gate, I noticed that my electrician buddy was wearing the squadron commander's gold-braided cap. After much discussion, it was decided to hide the hat in the locker in the motor room below the maneuvering room. We hoped that no one saw us come aboard.

"We were rousted out to quarters at 0900 where the squadron commander announced all liberty was canceled until his hat was returned. After muster, a private conversation took place during a meeting in the motor room, where it was decided that the hat would be hidden in a dirty pillow case with the laundry, then taken past the sleeping Lieutenant Cunningham, to his car outside the gate.

"Before an hour had passed, it was announced that liberty would resume at 1300. No harm was done, but I never got up the nerve to ask Lieutenant Cunningham who found the hat and who got chewed out. So that ended that. But whenever I have a beer at Sub Vet reunions, I think about my buddies who went down with her," Greenwood said.

Kangaroo Express

About the time that the crippled *Growler* was heading back to Brisbane, the fortune of the Japanese land acquisitions was being reversed on Guadalcanal. By the end of February, Army troops under the command of Maj. Gen. Alexander M. Patch had cleared the island of Japanese troops after six months of bitter fighting by Marine and Army units. Under the command of Schade, *Growler* was passing by with her nose all bent out of shape.

On her fifth war patrol, the first after the almost fatal ramming of the *Hayasaki,* the *Kangaroo Express* as *Growler* was affectionately called by this time, departed Brisbane 13 May 1943 for the Solomon Islands where fierce battles were taking place.

Charles P. Trumbull served in *Growler* during her fifth through her ninth war patrols—the last three as torpedo and gunnery officer. He was a 1941 graduate of the Naval Academy and served a year and a half aboard the heavy cruiser USS *Louisville* prior to attending Submarine School from September to December 1942.

According to Trumbull, "In my class were Lt. Richard K. Mason, class of 1940, and Lt. j.g. Norman Naylor, class of 1943. After finishing Sub School, I was ordered to Brisbane to await assignment to a boat. After two or three months of serving on relief crews there, I was ordered to the *Growler* along with Mason and Naylor. We were joined by Lt. j.g. Harry Messick, a mustang a few years older than Schade, and who had served in S-boats off China for many years. Messick had yet to make a war patrol. The *Growler* had recently lost Gilmore and Ensign Williams. Lt. Landon Davis was transferred to new construction shortly and after, and Lt. Jack Cunningham was ordered to an R-boat in Key West. So *Growler* needed four new officers, and we greenhorns were it."

Lt. Comdr. Arnold F. Schade was in command. Adding to her reputation, in the course of the patrol *Growler* attacked and sank the 5,200-ton *Miyandono Maru. Growler* was clearly gaining a distinction for its daring successes, which was even acknowledged by the infamous "Tokyo Rose."

Excerpts from the now declassified war patrol reports written by Skipper Schade read:

> GROWLER—report of fifth war patrol—period from 15 May 1943 to 30 June, 1943:

(A) PROLOGUE.

> GROWLER returned to port on 17 February with the bow seriously damaged as a result of ramming an enemy gunboat. Repairs were effected and a new bow was built by Evans Deakin Company of Brisbane, Australia after determining that no marked damage was suffered by the tubes. The U.S.S. FULTON began a regular refit, completely overhauling #3 Main Engine. All new main and crank bearings were installed in #3 and #4 Main Engines. Submarine base Brisbane, Australia built a 4" platform on the conning tower and built a 20 m.m. platform forward end of the bridge....On 1 May 1943, ship was undocked with most of the bow complete. Test firing, using dummy torpedoes, was conducted alongside the tender. On 5 May operated in Moreton Bay. Fired exercise torpedoes from the bow tubes. On 6 May tested and fired all guns. Operated at sea for training from 7 May until 11 May. Proceed on patrol on 13 May, conducting training enroute.

B. NARRATIVE:

14 May 1943:

2000	Escort departed.	
	Noon position: 25-41 S.	Miles steamed 228
	155-35 E.	Fuel used 2194 gal.

15 May 1943:

	Noon position: 22-07 S.	Miles steamed 221.1
	156-11 E.	Fuel used 2003 gal.

16 May 1943:

	Noon position: 17-42 S.	Miles steamed 260
	156-22 E.	Fuel used 2457 gal.

Trumbull relates "the matter of flying fish. On my first patrol standing the 04–08 watch, I discovered that on many mornings there would be a good number of flying fish which had landed on deck during the night. Getting permission to go on deck while the navigator was taking his stars, I would scoop up as many as I could and deposit them in the wardroom fridge. Of course, I had never heard of eating flying fish but I soon discovered that they were my very favorite seafood, gutted, scaled and sautéed in butter they made a great breakfast! I later found that flying fish were a favorite item in all restaurants of Barbados. Flying fish are great gliders.

Swimming at top speed they come out of the water sculling furiously with their elongated lower tail. As they lose altitude, and if they hit a wave right, they can again scull like mad and take off again without actually reentering the water.

"I have timed them in the air for over thirty seconds, and they attain some unbelievable heights. While standing a nighttime bridge watch in Japanese waters with all the watch quietly peering through binoculars, suddenly —wham!!—a flying fish would hit the superstructure right alongside you. One night the OOD, Harry Messick, was hit in the eye by one and went around with a black eye for some days. The height of eye above the surface was seventeen feet (the height used for star sight calculations), so it was thereby proved that flying fish can soar at least up to seventeen feet."

17 May 1943:

        Noon position: 13-27 S.   Miles steamed 271.
                   156-51 E.   Fuel used 2427 gal.

18 May 1943:

        Noon position: 9-34 S.   Miles steamed 225
                   156-38 E.   Fuel used 2380 gal.

    1410   Position: 9-28.5 S. 156-41.5 E.
Sighted unidentified patrol plane on easterly course. Flying low. <u>PLANE CONTACT #1</u>

20 May 1943:

    0045   Position: 6-25 S. 153-59 E
While proceeding north along neutral lane, in full bright moon light with a very hazy horizon, the OOD aft and a lookout both reported a large submarine close aboard (2000 yards). Radar not in use since the bright moon deceived us as to visibility. Believe he saw us at the same time. Both subs started turning. We submerged, but could make no sound contact.

On 22 May 1943 *Growler* entered assigned area from eastern boundary about 2400. She had traveled 2078 nautical miles to her assigned area, consuming 19,462 gallons of fuel. There were 74,577 gallons remaining.

Except for a futile two-hour chase of four ships in formation, the next few days were uneventful except for some mechanical problems.

Then on the 28th, several distant heavy explosions were heard. *Growler* had spent four days in covering the spot recommended by the *Grayback*, and two days covering the *Albacore's* spot without seeing even a ripple on the glassy seas.

Skipper Schade believed that these areas were being avoided, so he decided to head for Polows–Rabaul traffic lanes off Rambutyo to find a "heavy corner of our own."

Around midnight of the 4th of June *Growler* sighted a ship bearing 307° about eight miles distant. Closed at high speeds but at 8,000 yards the target zigged away towards Tingwon Island. It was very disappointing to miss this shot as the vessel was identified as similar to a *Takatiho Maru* class, a very large ship. But as the area seemed to be a good spot where ships appear to pass through, unescorted at high speeds, Schade decided to stay.

Shortly after midnight on a dark, moonless night with calm seas and no horizon, a large patrol boat or a destroyer was sighted fairly close abeam to port. *Growler* was headed south patrolling at three knots with radar out of commission. *Growler* turned away at full speed on all four engines. The target appeared to have headed away.

Two weeks later, Skipper Schade recorded in his report that "destroyers patrolling at high speed indicates that ships are probably to the northeast heading for Rabaul with reinforcements, supplies and equipment. It also indicated that one of the American subs had been detected. *Growler* surfaced and headed southeast to chase and gain attack position on the enemy ships. She obtained course and speed data from *Greenling* and headed for daylight position of convoy."

19 June 1943:

0705	Sighted smoke bearing 298° T. Ships apparently headed south west. Unable to close. Decided to open and surface. <u>CONTACT #15-26.</u>
0951	Sighted submarine on surface bearing 30° T., speed 17 knots, course 200° T. We hoped it would be enemy but recognized GREENLING. Exchanged smoke bomb signals, surfaced and started chasing convoy.
1130	With convoy smoke in plain sight, ships turned to northeast and tops came over fast. Submerged. GREENLING continued.
1235	Convoy back on southerly course. Surfaced on all main engines, 18.5 knots. Kept tops in sight and at
1438	Submerged ahead of ships for attack. Their zigs were incomprehensible causing us to run at full speed most of the time to stay in front.
1616	COMMENCED FIRING. Fired four fish at largest ship, similar to ZUIXO MARU, 60 port track, range 1000 yards, gyros 1L, 1R, 4L, 4R. Fired two fish at second vessel, similar to TAITO MARU, 90° port track, range 2000 yards, gyros 0°, 2R. Obtained two hits on each target. Sound heard all fish run normal; explosions heard, checking with time of run. Only observed hit was first on large MARU. We were directly in front of another MARU and an escort and started down immediately. Sounds of breaking up and interval explosions were heard from the smallest vessel.

> 1619   Depth charge attack began. This was the most severe ever
> experienced by this vessel. First run, he came over ping-
> ing, dropped 11 depth charges. On all subsequent runs
> he would locate us by pinging and listening, proceed to
> position directly overhead and stop. He may have had some
> sort of magnetic indicator. After determining our direc-
> tion he would drop a small salvo of 1 to 3 charges;
> all of these appeared to be extremely close. Much minor
> damage incurred. Forward gyro regulator went out, firing
> circuits out forward and aft. Holding down clamps both
> sound heads carried away. Pit log out. Many instruments lights
> and compartment lights out. In view of the trouble with TDC and
> firing circuits, it was decided not to trail the convoy.

Growler surfaced in black stormy sea and sighted a large *Maru* dead in the water smoking heavily, with a two other ships standing by. Sent message to headquarters regarding attack.

The next morning *Growler* sighted smoke and closed for attack. But because of a nearby escort, which closed, she was unable to give chase. The destroyer remained in the area for several hours, requiring *Growler* to use evasive measures at periscope depth. Thereafter she lost all contact.

On 21 June *Growler* left the area. She had steamed 1,303 miles in the area using 22,565 gallons of fuel. Heading back to Brisbane *Growler* sighted one "Betty" on patrol and detected numerous pingings which were anti-sub patrols. An Allied bomber dropped three bombs reporting *Growler* as a Jap sub. She encountered very heavy seas. The forward 20 mm gun platform was carried away.

After having steamed 2033 nautical miles from her station she had consumed 22,420 gallons of fuel. The *Kangaroo Express* arrived Brisbane, Queensland on the 30th of June 1943 after forty-seven days on her fifth war patrol.

In the "first endorsement to the commanding officer *Growler* report of fifth war patrol," the commander of submarine squadron eight stated that the patrol was conducted under the command of Schade, and was "highlighted by the aggressive chase and attack on a southbound convoy, two hits being obtained on each of two ships.

"It is recommended that the *Growler* be credited with sinking one passenger freighter of 4,467 tons, and severely damaging a freighter tanker of 7,360 tons."

Growler had, by postwar reports, actually sunk the 5,300 ton *Miyadono Maru*, which Tokyo Rose had previously mentioned.

The second endorsement by Adm. James Fife stated that "the fifth patrol of the *Growler*, which was the first for her present commanding officer, was conducted in a skillful and aggressive manner. The attack on the convoy, which was well escorted and was commanded by a Jap who knew his business, was especially well conducted. It is believed that both ships which were attacked eventually sank. The larger of the two was observed dead in the water and smoking heavily more than two hours after the attack. *Guardfish* who trailed the convoy for two hours after *Growler*'s attack, reported counting only four ships in it when contact was lost in heavy rain.

"The depth charge attack tactics employed by the convoy escort indicate that the enemy has an effective use of some means whereby the anti-submarine vessel can determine when it is directly over a submarine. It is therefore logical to assume that the enemy has developed a magnetic indicator similar to our own, and it may be that he has found useful for hovering. Such tactics are not ordinarily employed by our own antisubmarine vessels which utilize the magnetic indicator only as a guide to a 'drop' time after high speed approach with echo-ranging. Enemy depth-charge attack methods are definitely more effective at present than they were a year ago. The only answer to the small escort vessel currently and effectively used in this area is gunfire when guns are installed on submarines which will outrange the Jap.

"There are more and more indications of enemy shipboard radar installations and the use of the submarine as a night torpedo boat is on the wane. Our submarines should all have efficient radar detectors installed in order that they may determine when it is advisable to attempt night surface attacks and when not. Without such detectors it is only a matter of time until our submarines will have to abandon night surface attacks altogether in order to avoid falling into radar' traps and being sunk by surprise gunfire. At present less than half of the submarines of this task force are equipped with detectors. Equipment has been requested and it is expected that all will be so equipped within the next six months."

Admiral Fife's endorsement of *Growler*'s highly successful fifth war patrol ended with, "A job well done."

This was Leonard Greenwood's last patrol on the *Growler*. In July, Greenwood was returned to the United States for reassignment. On 19 February 1944, at Portsmouth, New Hampshire, he joined the newly commissioned USS *Pomfret* (SS 391).

Pomfret's skipper was Frank Clements. In October of 1944 Acker became disabled and gave his executive officer, Frederic Clarke command of the boat. Ordered to Saipan, *Pomfret* came upon a large force of ships. Acker took back his command to sink a large transport, the *Tsuyama Maru* of 6,962 tons.

Leonard Greenwood completed six war patrols on *Pomfret,* the last ending in August of 1945 when World War II ended. His final patrol lasted fifty-nine days in the East China Sea under Skipper John B. Hess.

Leonard Greenwood listed some things a wartime submariner never forgets:

- the order to secure battle stations and that shot of whisky.
- The firing of the first torpedo at the enemy.
- The explosion of hits and misses on the target.
- The almost certain depth-charge attacks that followed.
- The experience of near misses and the damage done.
- The breaking up noises of sinking targets from pressure.
- The mental and physical closeness of your mates.
- The smell of combined body odors and diesel.
- The smell of combined cooked food, stale air and diesel fumes.
- The combined odors of all above plus lead-acid batteries.

Then there were good things that happened. More of a diversion. There were torpedo and anchor pools with each man donating two dollars for a

Leonard Greenwood, June 1943 in Pearl Harbor.

total of a hundred dollars or more. The two winners were the man closest to the first torpedo hit and the minute of the first line over at the end of a patrol.

Greenwood considered his first watch change to the starboard (junior) side of the controllers in the maneuvering room, the senior man (port side) taught him more than the books he studied. The result was passing the test for earning his dolphins (qualified submariner) and 3rd Class Electrician Mate rating. Now that's true dedication! Studying off watch while fulfilling his other duties was considered a great accomplishment. And that it was!

Other good events were just making it to port on empty fuel tanks. Having used 118,000 gallons of diesel on one long patrol, the *Growler* barely made it back to port. Tying up in Brisbane, Australia, after having left the *Fulton* at Midway in September, three months earlier, to see old buddies was a highlight. Not least of all, the rest and recuperation he had in Australia was a very good thing.

The bad happenings he listed included being bombed by B-24 Liberators, ill feelings he had for a shipmate who stole from him, the foul air due to the lack of oxygen after being submerged for twelve to fourteen hours, no water for a bath, and on and on, ad nauseam.

Moby Dick

The Bismarck Sea is part of the southwestern pacific ocean. It lies between the northeastern coast of New Guinea and the Islands of the Bismarck Archipelago. The sea extends about five hundred miles east and west. Bismarck Archipelago consists of more than three hundred islands just north of the Equator. The two largest islands are New Britain and New Ireland. The group also includes the Admiralty Islands. Germany occupied the unclaimed islands in 1884 and Australian troops captured them during the First World War. As a result, the League of Nations mandated the islands to Australia in 1920. In 1942 the Japanese Imperial Army sized the islands and established army and naval bases in this strategic area. Rabaul was a major base from which ships, troops and war material sailed down The Slot during the battle for Guadalcanal in 1942 and 1943, according to numerous sources.

Between 2 and 5 March 1943, the Allied Forces of the United States, Britain and Holland defeated a Japanese naval force in the Battle of the Bismarck Sea. While General MacArthur's land campaign was in full swing, allied naval forces caught a major Japanese convoy of reinforcements and war supplies bound for Lae, New Guinea. Allied Navy and Air Force attacks virtually destroyed the enemy convoy. At battle's end, the Japanese had lost 15,000 men and 90,000 tons of supplies. The Japanese had also lost 63 of their 150 Zero air cover.

In July of 1942 Admiral King agreed that once Guadalcanal had been secured, the advance to Rabaul would fall under General MacArthur's command. The advance to Rabaul, which was part of the "Tokyo Express," began 5 July in the Kula Gulf and ended on the 2nd of November in the Battle of Empress Augusta Bay. Rabaul was bypassed to "wither on the vine."

Skipper Schade's *Kangaroo Express* departed Brisbane 21 July 1943 for the Bismarck sea on its sixth patrol. It lasted for fifty-three days, of which thirty-seven were spent in the combat area.

Trumbull relates a very scary experience not in the war patrol reports. "After finishing refits there [Brisbane], boats were required to submerge in the river nearby the tender and lie on the bottom with the main ballast tank vents open while the division commander in a row boat inspected the surface over the boat for any air bubbles rising to the surface, which would indicate a leak somewhere in the high-pressure air bottles located in the tanks. This we did. While lying on the bottom the skipper decided to make 'battle surface' and man the deck gun, so when we got the signal that the inspection was over the order was passed to prepare for battle surface. This requires putting a lot of people in the conning tower: in addition to the skipper, the officer of the deck, and the junior officer of the deck, the three lookouts, the quartermaster, and the radar operator required for a normal surfacing, there were the gun crew of trainer, pointer, loader, gun captain (me) and ammunition passers. So we were packed in like sardines."

Trumbull continued, "On the order to surface, the man on the air manifolds blows the tanks. Unfortunately, neither the chief on the hydraulic manifold, which controls the vents, nor the diving officer remembered that the vents were still open. The high-pressure air rushed into the tanks fast enough to blow them dry in spite of the vents being open, and upon surfacing the skipper sprung the hatch open and rushed to the bridge. He was the only one who made it. The air in the tanks was vented and the boat submerged with Schade busy climbing the periscope shears. The conning tower hatch was held open by a latch, which was released by pulling a lanyard, which then pulled the hatch closed. The water was pouring down the open hatch with such force that the quartermaster could not find and grasp the lanyard.

"Meanwhile the rest of us were standing with our arms pinned to our sides praying that Wagner could find that thing. With the water pouring down into the control room, the diving officer pulled shut the hatch between the two compartments, leaving us trapped in the conning tower. After what seemed like an eternity but was probably just a matter of seconds, Wagner found the lanyard and closed the hatch while we onlookers stood in water almost to our armpits. Down in the control room they finally realized what the problem was and reblew the tanks and the boat resurfaced. It was a scary experience."

Robert A. Link was born 2 February 1923, in Atlantic City, New Jersey, the second of nine children. At the age of ten he saw the movie *Hell Below,* about a World War I submarine. He knew then that he would some day be a submariner.

Just after the Japanese attack on Pearl Harbor, Link enlisted in the Navy, volunteering for service in the submarine force. After boot camp, he attended the submarine school at New London, Connecticut. By the end of 1942, he was in Brisbane, Australia. His first assignment was on the USS *Grayback*. Link served on *Grayback* on one war patrol and when it returned to Brisbane, he transferred to *Growler* on which he served the sixth, seventh and eighth patrols.

Robert A. "Bob" Link, April 1944.

Link's proudest moment of his life was the time was when he qualified as a submariner aboard the *Kangaroo Express* in late 1943. His experiences are his best recollections of a time long ago. Link went aboard *Growler* in spring of 1943 as F 2/c and was assigned to the auxiliary gang. According to Link, this is that part of the crew that gets to do all of the dirty work aboard ship in port or out at sea. Being the lowest man on the auxiliary pole meant that he'd have to clean the head. Now, this is real *esprit de corps* when a man is proud to do the worst jobs.

In addition, the auxiliary gang was responsible for the maintenance of most machinery located in the pump room, i.e. compressors, pumps, lathes, condensers, blowers, high and low pressure, and manifolds. The auxiliary gang did not stand engine room watches, except, perhaps as an emergency.

Link considered himself fortunate that most of his time was spent on lookout watches or on bow and stern planes. But lookout watches were plainly dangerous. So why does a man volunteer for something that puts him at personal risk? Heroes are like that.

In an incident following her overhaul, while alongside the tender *Fulton*, *Growler* cast off her lines and centered in the Brisbane River for a test dive, dropping to the bottom—perhaps forty feet. Watertight integrity was checked throughout the ship.

The order was given to "surface the boat." Instead, as Link recounted, "air was applied to the ballast tanks and we surfaced. The conning tower hatch was opened and the men there went onto the bridge. The air banks were secured and with that *Growler* settled back down to the bottom of the river. The pump room directly under the control room was flooded before the hatch was closed. Two men had been stranded on the bridge. This had all been caused by ballast tank vents not having been properly closed prior to surfacing." Being the new man on board without an assigned station, Link stood clear of traffic, probably wondering about his fate. The end result was that the crew got a few extra days in port to clean up the mess.

Kangaroo Express then went on her sixth patrol centering on the Solomon Islands, New Britain, and New Ireland. There were mostly aircraft contacts and diving and surfacing with no torpedoes expended. She then went back to Brisbane for a tune-up.

Growler's first five days were spent in training while proceeding in company with *Tuna*, *Silversides* and *Coucal* from Brisbane to the Louisiades where she refueled to capacity from *Coucal*. She arrived in her area north of New Ireland on 30 July 1943. On the following day she made an unsuccessful torpedo attack on an armed trawler of about 1,500 tons, which was towing a large barge toward Wewak.

From 6 August to 26 August the *Kangaroo Express* was on a submarine scouting line south of Truk. During this period she had numerous plane contacts but only three ship contacts. Two of the latter were patrol craft, and the third was with a northbound hospital ship. It was common knowledge that the Japanese, in violation of the Geneva Convention prohibiting attacks on ships marked with a Red Cross, were transporting troops and war materiel on them. Nevertheless, American warships honored the Geneva Convention and did not attack hospital ships.

Skipper Schade made the following entries in his report:

21 August 1943:
    0928   PLANE CONTACT #17. Submerged, plane contact by radar. Two planes were beamed on our SD giving two large steady "pips." Position: 4-43 N. 151-12 E.

22 August 1943:
    0817   Submerged for bad weather, poor visibility
    1110   PLANE CONTACT #18. Sighted through periscope one "Mavis" patrol plane, flying low, course north. Position: 4-50 N. 152-22 E.

23 August 1943:
    1600   FISH STORY #1. Ran into school of blackfish. Hit one head on, with severe jar. Ran over him and cut him up with the propellers. Left a large pool of blood and fish chunks. No apparent damage.

Trumbull said, "According to Harry Messick, who was the officer of the deck, several whales, or blackfish (blackfish are one type of whale), were cavorting nearby. Suddenly one of them, presumably the bull, turned and rammed us head on, maybe thinking we were a threat to his harem."

24 August 1943:
    1000   PLANE CONTACT #19. Submerged for plane contact by radar, 20 miles, closing.
    1426   PLANE CONTACT #20. Sighted one "Mavis" patrol plane, 3 miles, flying very low. Position: 2-57 N. 152-27 E.

25 August 1943:
    1915   SHIP CONTACT #4. Sighted hospital ship properly lighted, course north, speed 12 knots. Position: 4-00 N. 151-24 E.

26 August 1943:
    0400   Sounded off, prior to leaving patrol line.
    0635   PLANE CONTACT #21. Radar indications, two planes, 4 to 12 miles. Position: 3-20 N.151-40 E.

27 August 1943:
    1920   Sighted four searchlights from KAVIENG, distant 135 miles.

6 September 1943:
                FISH STORY #2. Upon surfacing the deck was found covered with large Bonita fish. We collected a large sack full (over fifty) and served fresh fillet to all hands.

Link's fish story was duly noted in Skipper Schade's patrol report of the 6 September 1943. According to Link, "The standard operating procedure (SOP) was to dive before daylight and surface after sundown to recharge the batteries. Surfacing soon after dark also meant getting the best star shots for the navigator." One night when Link was standing as lookout on the surface behind the quartermaster who had followed the officer of the deck (OD) and climbing the lower ladder to the lookout stand, he was shaken by an ungodly expletive behind his back. "I can't describe the terror that I felt for a second but when I turned forward to find the deck covered with fish of all sizes, I felt good in knowing that mess cooks on deck with bags guaranteed fresh fish on the menu for the crews' evening chow."

Trumbull recalls the event: "We surfaced one evening and after getting to the bridge, Skipper Schade yelled down for some men to get to the top side on the double. Bringing with them burlap sacks used to store garbage in during the day."

Trumbull was on deck at the time and directed the collection of the 'fat fish' into the burlap bags. "We had surfaced in a large school of bonitos and several dozen were flopping around on the deck. *Growler* at that time had the old wood deck—slats of wood with one-inch spaces between them, rather than the perforated steel deck. With the latter, the water on surfacing would have run off the sides, taking the fish with it. With the wood deck the water ran down between the slats, which thus served as a net, leaving the fish high and dry. Of course some managed to flop themselves over the side. But twenty-three were bagged and provided for a large fish dinner the next night."

When the scouting line was discontinued on 26 August, *Growler* proceeded to the vicinity of New Hanover, where she spent ten days and had four contacts: one with a medium freighter that she was unable to close; a hospital ship; another, a gunboat which passed out of range; and one brief encounter with an unidentified ship which was lost in a rain squall. *Growler* returned to Brisbane via the bombing restriction lane east of the Solomons, arriving 12 September 1943.

Admiral Fife commented in his endorsement of *Growler*'s sixth war patrol that despite the lack of opportunities on this patrol, morale was high. Further, the patrol was remarkably free from material derangements, which in fact reflects favorable credit on both *Growler* and *Fulton*.

According to the endorsement of commander submarine squadron eight, *Growler* suffered no material casualties while on patrol. The main storage battery was in poor condition. It had been necessary to disconnect six cells in the forward battery due to grounds. This battery had jars with steel inserts and iron contamination was prevalent. During the refit in September all showing signs of iron were flushed and new acid added. No attempt was to be made at that time to replace the six defective cells because of the time required and the fact that *Growler* was scheduled to return to the United States for a Navy yard overhaul upon completion of her next patrol. The *Growler* was then given a regular refit by the *Fulton*.

"Charlie! Charlie!"

Jap Zeroes coming in out of the sun were impossible to see when on the surface. As was so often in the later days of the war, American subs wanting the greater speed on the surface were at risk to the "Charlies," as they were called. *Growler* was no exception. Amphibious landings were preceded by submarine reconnaissance or by advance scouting parties landed by submarine, or both. The number of enemy fleet units in the Solomon-Bismarck-New Guinea area fluctuated as the Japanese ran occasional task groups down from Truk to reinforce the Eighth Fleet based at Rabaul. Coast watchers stationed by submarines in the upper Solomons and Bismarcks furnished much valuable information on enemy ship movements.

Admiral Halsey's Third Fleet had began its drive for the Solomons on 30 June 1943, with the capture of Rendova Island. To the north, New Georgia was next when the Army and Marines landed there on the 4th of July. In the next few days forces entered the Kula Gulf and an attack on Kolombangara Island. The Japanese, in a desperate attempt to save New Georgia sent in seven destroyers from Bougainville which were quickly routed by U.S. forces.

Alarmed by the subsequent defeat at Bougainville, the Japanese high command dispatched part of Admiral Kurita's Second Fleet to the Solomon-Bismarck front from Truk. A follow-through punch at Rabaul made any hope for the Japanese to reinforce Bougainville a waste. The 27,000 troops there were isolated and out of action. The battle for the upper Solomons was effectively over.

The deployment of submarines during this period to head off Admiral Kuritas's Second Fleet, which sortied down from Truk, was mainly ineffective. *Growler* was stationed closest to Truk had been forced to leave its station because of severe problems just before Kurita's cruisers sortied. In any event, even had *Growler* been there, they probably would have traveled on another passage, undetected, to Rabaul.

On her seventh war patrol, out of Brisbane, from the 4th of October 1943 to 7 November 1943, *Growler* conducted actions in the Solomons-Bismarck sea area despite a major problem with her storage batteries. She proceeded to sea in company with *Coucal*, *Balao* and *Silversides*.

9 October 1943:

0715   Met SC 729 and proceeded to TULAGI. Fueled to capacity (18,704 gals.). During the day contacted numerous planes, not listed under contacts. During the fueling, air raid alarm sounded and GROWLER got under way; 10 minutes later all-clear sounded.

1845   Arrived on station 1,679 miles from Brisbane.

10 October 1943:

0717   <u>PLANE CONTACT #1</u>. Sighted bearing 105°, ten miles. Course North, probably a Liberator.

0823   <u>PLANE CONTACT #2.</u> Sighted Jap "Mavis", plainly marked, circling overhead about 1000'. Position: 6-42 S.159.03 E. (Off New Guinea about four hundred miles below the equator.)

1032   <u>PLANE CONTACT #3</u>. Two planes, one seen clearly to be a "Mavis." We were heavily strafed at 35'. Acquired a few more MG and cannon holes in the bridge. TBT aft partially shot away.

Trumbull's recollection of this incident was that as officer of the deck, "Ensign Walter Smith was junior officer of the deck aft. We were on the surface proceeding at a good speed. Calm sea, bright sun. Suddenly Smith began yelling 'Charlie! Charlie!' and at the same time the SJ radar operator yelled 'Aircraft contact!'

"I dove. The planes came in from dead astern directly out of the sun so weren"t seen until close. As I was closing the hatch I could hear the bullets, one exploding on the hatch, a foot or two over my head, but of course on the other side of the hatch. Upon surfacing shortly afterwards I picked up my pieces of the shell that had hit the hatch and saved them for many years in a razorblade box. Many bullet holes were seen in the bridge plating."

12 October 1943:

    Entered WIDE BAY, NEW BRITAIN. Found nothing in the bay.

18 October 1943:

0145   <u>SHIP CONTACT #4.</u> Sighted smoke.....Determined course.

0600   Submerged ahead for attack....Having fired at identical ships twice before with negative results, did not attack. Escort passed so close astern could see only grey paint in low power, but he did not detect us.

Link remembers that when the USS *Growler* departed Brisbane on her seventh war patrol, she was assigned to the same area as she had been on her sixth patrol, the Solomons–Bismarck Sea area extending towards Truk Island. During this patrol the *Kangaroo Express* suffered a severe fire in the maneuvering room, which was actually the control center of the ship's propulsion. *Growler* had by now been at sea since early 1942—at Midway, the Aleutians, the China Sea and a nasty near disastrous encounter with a Japanese warboat. She had also suffered an incident that left her with a squeak in one of her main drive shafts, and was long due for a major overhaul.

As Link put it, "*Kangaroo Express* was ordered back to the United States. But not before being caught on the surface it the early morning by two Japanese patrol planes and severely strafed. I recall that I had come off watch at 8:00 A.M. and was asleep in my bunk when I was awakened by the diving alarm and a tattooing coming through the hull. In a few moments with no further ado coming from the control room I drifted back off to sleep. It was when I awoke for noon chow that I learned that we had been strafed. That's the way it was in submarines. For what purpose should the entire crew have been called to general quarters? We stayed down the rest of the day, proceeding to Pearl Harbor to off-load torpedoes and excess materials. At this time the crew was awarded combat pins for the first time. I received mine for the successful patrol I had made on board *Grayback* in early 1943."

Lieutenant Trumbull being awarded the Navy Commendation Medal in Pearl Harbor for his fifth war patrol by Commodore Comstock.

26 October 1943:

> Condition of main generators and storage battery has become progressively worse....

2145
> Fire in main control cubicle. Lost all power....Began withdrawing from TRUK on one port engine.

27 October 1943:

0230
> Received CTF-72 message telling us to head towards Pearl.

0800
> Submerged to make repairs.

28 October 1943:

> Left station - miles steamed on station - 2601.

7 November, 1943:

> Met SC 983 - escorted into Pearl.

Schade's report at the end of the patrol indicated "the crew's morale was high and their performance was excellent. Many 'old timers' remained. The limiting factor of this patrol was the progressively poor condition of the main storage battery and the main generators, with excessive grounds, which caused the patrol to be cut short."

Endorsements of *Growler*'s seventh patrol stated that she had to leave the area early due to material casualties and a poor storage battery. It also acknowledged that good area coverage was conducted during the patrol.

Photo courtesy of Charles Trumbull.

Lieutenant Trumbull after the seventh war patrol in Waikiki, Hawaii, November 1943.

This strategic employment of submarines in scouting below Truk came as a result of Admiral Halsey staff's assessment. Unfortunately, the deployment was a zero accomplishment which emphasized submarines' limitations in open-sea scouting.

But *Growler* was in need of extensive work. She was ordered to leave her battle station and proceed to Pearl Harbor. From there, Skipper Schade was given instructions to take *Growler* to the U.S. Navy yard at Hunter's Point, California. Any vehicle driven as hard as *Growler* had been, was in need for an extensive overhaul and as Trumbull said, "the bridge plating was replaced with bulletproof steel."

After overhaul at Hunter's Point, California, we made diving tests in San Francisco Bay. Link was standing directly under the main ballast vent, in the after battery. When the dive klaxon sounded, the vents opened and the connecting arm "over my head came into view through the oil drip pan. I saw that had been installed backwards.

Photo courtesy of the Kangaroo Express.

January 1944. Skipper Schade and his wife, Becky, relax with William Farmer in San Francisco while Growler *gets a complete overhaul at Hunter's Point.*

"For a split second I saw tons of water coming through the hull and I was on the receiving end. There might just as well been a cause—I knew I was a goner."

Link had been promoted to first class in late 1943 after *Kangaroo Express*'s seventh war patrol. Although at that time there was not a MOMM

Members of the Growler *crew enjoy liberty during the extensive overhaul
in San Francisco during the winter of 1943–44. Above, l. to r.: Harold Creeger,
Leville, Paul McGloughlin, Wright and Norman Lassiter.
Below, Art Ullrich (l.) and Milton Weymouth.*

third-class rating or stripe, you did get third-class pay. In early 1944 BU-
PERS authorized a third-class rating and stripe for MOMM 3/c. The yeo-
man notified all concerned that they could sew on a crow. Link said, "I first
displayed mine at the ship's dance, and Skipper Schade, while on the dance
floor, asked me what was that I had on my sleeve. Curious that he not had
been informed, I often wondered how other F 3/c's got the word." This is
yet another example of how much pride there was in the "Silent Service."

Typhoon

When asked about escaping the fury of a typhoon, Skipper Schade simply says "run deep!" But as even he will admit, you don't always have that choice. Often you must battle your enemy on the surface. Such was the case off Japan's southern coast in early 1944. Returning to the Pacific in February 1944, *Growler* departed from Pearl Harbor. After refueling at Midway, Schade headed for *Growler*'s new patrol assignment in the East China Sea. This would be Schade's eighth war patrol and his last on the *Kangaroo Express*.

USS Growler (SS 215), *departing San Francisco, February of 1944 on her eighth war patrol, which was Skipper Schade's last as her commander.*

Skipper Schade's report read:

(A) <u>Prologue</u>:

> On 18 November 1943, GROWLER began Navy Yard overhaul at Hunter's Point, California. Major items of repair include renewal of all battery jars, installation of skewed slot main motors, repairs of all main generators, installation of SJI-PPI radar, JP sound, Berkeley trim pump, raising #1 periscope to conning tower and rebuilding the bridge using BPS.

> Arrived Pearl Harbor 8 February 1944, following post repair trials, sound test, deperming. Conducted training and tests at Pearl. Departed 21 February 1944 for patrol with stop at Midway.

(B) <u>NARRATIVE</u>:

25 February 1944:

> 1030   Arrived Midway. Effected repairs to both auxiliary engines, Main Motor bearings, and storage battery grounds caused by opening of the jars due to heavy seas.

26 February 1944:

> 0800   Departed Midway.

28 February 1944:

> #1 Auxiliary Engine out of commission for the remainder of patrol.

A week out of Midway, *Growler* encountered a fierce typhoon. The storm's violent winds and high seas delayed her arrival in the East China Sea, south of Japan's coast.

The surface battle against Japan had now moved from the Gilbert Islands into the Marshall Islands. Unlike the Gilberts, which the Japanese had occupied at the outbreak of the war, the Marshalls had been in Japanese hands since the Versailles Treaty mandates after World War I. Against strong urging by his staff, Admiral Nimitz decided that the next major assault would be against Kwajalein.

Kwajalein is the world's largest coral atoll and hosted strategic Japanese military facilities. Nimitz's decision to take Kwajalien proved to be right. It was an effective land attack by Marines and Army troops. And it was along the lines of the original "Plan Orange," only it was taking longer than expected. The invasion was so successful that Admiral King decided to bypass the Carolines altogether and leap 1,200 miles to the west to the Marianas' Ring of Defense to Japan.

Growler, in the meantime was making its way to the East China Sea. This course carried it, as the crow flies, far north of the actions in the Marshalls, ostensibly to cut off traffic to the southern Japanese defenses.

Again, Schade's dairy describes the difficulties that were plaguing *Growler*:

3 March 1944:

    0140   In extremely rough weather. A tremendous wave carried over the bridge. Much water in all compartments from control to after engine room. Cruising in heavy weather with #4 MBT filled with fuel is very troublesome, flooding the main induction frequently, and causing solid water to come through the conning tower hatch almost continuously. 1 engine speed - 5.5 knots; 2 engine speed—8.5 knots.

    2000   #4 Main Motor bearing burned out.

4 March 1944:   Seas mountainous. Port shaft still out of commission. Speed about four knots. Battery acid spilled, causing full voltage grounds.

    0845   Decided to submerge for a few hours to work on casualties.

5 March 1944:

    0800   Port shaft back in commission.

6 March 1944:

    1045   Taking continuous solid seas over the bridge. Submerged for three hours.

10 March 1944:

    1900   Arrived in area, three days late; caused by casualty to Main Motor bearing and unbroken stormy weather and heavy seas.

11 March 1944:   Periscope observations difficult at any speed.

12 March 1944:   Patrolled NE sector of AMAMI O SHIMA

13 March 1944:   Patrolled passage between AMAMI O SHIMA and YOKOATE

    0857   <u>CONTACT #1</u> Sighted small patrol craft, SC type, base course 350° T., speed nine knots.

14 March 1944:   Patrolled passage east of TORI SHIMA

    2330 I.   <u>CONTACT #2</u>. In bright moonlight sighted ship on the horizon, course south, speed 10 knots. Radar out of commission. Began end run to obtain attack position. While still at extreme range of visibility the ship turned toward us and started shooting. He turned away at 18 knots, but the target now seemed to be a very large destroyer, gained rapidly. With the shells falling too close for comfort, submerged. Prepared for a "down the throat" shot, but we were unable to hold to periscope depth, so went deep. He dropped depth charges over a period of an hour.

Charles Trumbull remembers: "Amami O Shima, about 120 miles off the Japanese Island of Kyoto, during March 1944. The weather is freezing, the seas, according to the patrol report are 'mountainous.' What made this really scary was that we couldn't get the hatch closed. We were of course at general quarters. The personnel on the bridge all wore heavy clothing.

"While clearing the bridge to dive the quartermaster had one of his mittens scooped off by one of the hatch dogs. It being night time the conning tower was lit only by a dim red light in order to preserve night vision.

The space under the hatch was almost in complete darkness. With the mitten covering the dog, the hatch couldn't be seated no matter how hard the quartermaster turned the dogging wheel, and nobody really knew what the problem was.

"Finally, just before the hatch was due go under, with an increasing amount of water pouring in, a white light was produced, the mitten observed and removed and the hatch dogged, just in the nick of time."

15 March 1944:

0415	Came to periscope depth. Could see nothing, although his pinging sounded close.
0430	Visibility closed in. Surfaced to open out, at high speed.
0445	CONTACT #3. With one destroyer astern sighted two more destroyers and two sub-chasers close aboard on starboard bow - about 3,000 yards. We began field running. Felt sure the first DD had detected us by radar. From 0740 to 0830 they dropped numerous depth charges in the area we had just vacated, about 8 - 10 miles south. During the day several more DC barrages were heard to the south of us.

20 March 1944:   Tried to enter passage south of KIKAI JIINA but found we had been sent east 20 miles.

22 March 1944:

0917   CONTACT #8. Sighted two small Marus, possibly 2000 T. Each, course 020°, speed 7 - 8 knots, close to shore. Unable to close; nearest range 7,000 yards.

1200	PLANE CONTACT #2. CONTACT #9. Sighted one "Pete" patrolling. Sighted a patrol boat heading southwest between TOKUNO and AMAMI O SHIMA.
1350	CONTACT #10. Sighted one small AK, 3,000 T. Course 030°, speed eight knots. Closed for attack.
1443	Fired four torpedoes aft, range 1700 yards, 2° divergent spread, depth set at 9 feet. Observed first wake which appeared to pass under the bow; others not seen. One possible hit at torpedo run at 1 minute - 36 seconds. Periscope ducked. Sound reported screws; went deep.

William L. Kuhl, a rightly nervous electronic technicians mate on *Kangaroo Express*'s eighth war patrol, described the attack of 22 March 1944:

1430	Ready all tubes aft.
1441	Ready 7....Fire 7! Ready 8....Fire 8! Ready 9....Fire 9! Ready 10 ...Fire 10!
1443	All fish missed, went under our target.
1446	Three depth charges.
1450	Six more charges.
1555	Eight more.
1457	Emergency lights on. Silent running. That one Nip up there is really close .... bearing 210° — going away.

	Bearing 205° 203° Coming in. 207. I guess we're still at 300 feet. 40,000 Skins out the window and only some jangled nerves to show for it.
1505	Wonder what's keeping our boys up there ???
1506	Six more charges—there's my answer. Further away now.
1515	Number one auxiliary was leaking. Secured. Rudder makes a lot of noise.
1525	Rudder again smoking lamp is out. Dinette is blue with smoke. Very warm and sticky in here.
1530	Three more charges. At 310 feet now. I'm glad now I didn't take a shower–I'd only be sweated up again. They're blowing number one auxiliary now. We can't get up–keep drifting down.
1540	I guess maybe that's all for this time from Tojo.
1546	Put bow planes in power. I'm on the battle phones now.

Except in his family's esteem, Kuhl was not a big man physically. Of average frame, blond hair, a baby face and relatively quiet, he was a hero of gigantic stature to his family. In those dark hours Kuhl calmly continued to record the battle raging above.

1547	We're going up to sixty feet now for a look. May I write "Fin" to this article??
1549	One more charge. Very far away probably meant for us though back down to 300 feet again.
1600	Six more, closer in now. Seems that they're moving in closer all the time.
1615	Down to 350 feet now.
1635	Still waiting..........
1640	Going up for another look.
1650	One more, along ways off. All we heard was a faint reverberation.
1700	Sixty-two feet. Just about over and done with, I hope.
1705	Open all W.T. doors and bulkhead ventilation flappers.
1715	Sighted another ship ... will we make an approach on it?
1720	Secure fire control party.

FIN

William Lewis Kuhl was a twenty-one-year-old native of Manitowoc, Wisconsin, who had enlisted in the Navy in 1942. After boot camp at San Diego, he attended various Navy schools to attain a proficiency in radio, radar and underwater sound equipment. Kuhl volunteered for the submarine service and was assigned to *Growler* at Mare Island, California, on 11 January 1944 as a radio technician. After completing his service aboard *Growler*, Kuhl served aboard submarine tenders *Sperry*, *Holland* and *Apollo* until the war's end.

22 March 1944 (continued):

      1445   Two patrol boats, not previously sighted, started depth charge attack.

1604   After 30 minutes of relative quiet started up to periscope
depth; at 170' depth charges started banging all around.   1700
Periscope depth. Four patrol boats in sight. Kept heading
away but they trailed right along.   1929
Surfaced about nine Miles from the beach. Nearest patrol
boat sighted astern about five miles. AMAMI O SHIMA
sparkled with blinding red lights, signal lights and an occasional searchlight. At the time we thought they had
picked us up, but apparently they were submarine
warning lights. Opened at high speed. The red lights were
still visible at 25 miles.

23 March 1944:

        PLANE CONTACT #3. Throughout the day we were escorted by one or more "Pete" planes plus patrol craft. We remained on evasive course, but at

      1815   The search culminated in a depth charge attack.
        At this time visibility was very poor but nothing was sighted close, so we remained at periscope depth. Not much chance to look for shipping.

25-27 March 1944:

        Patrolled to westward in continued rough seas, overcast stormy weather. Visibility 0-5 miles.

On the eighth patrol off Amami O Shima south of the Japanese main-land, one night was particularly black. The Pacific Ocean is spectacular at night because of phosphorous which lights the seas. On this night it was concentrated with a brilliant effect. This night, while *Growler* was on a battery-fuel combination, barely making rudder control, the area became highly illuminated. Usually, this was noted in the wake of the ship, but this time the entire area around the ship was like a pool of white and churning at the same time. Huge globules of the stuff gave the impression of being in a snow drift. The OD ordered a few more turns on the screws and *Growler* moved out of the area. It was a glorious mystical experience.

In the vicinity of Amami O Shima, riding on surface at battery motor combination, radar picked up a blip dead astern. The order came to all-stop and the chief soundman was called to the conning tower.

According to Link, "Moments of silence elapsed before he was asked what was heard astern the chief answered, 'Just our own screws, sir.' The order was that we were to remain at all stop. Then word came from the lookout. At the aft station that the target was signalling us. The next shouted warnings were 'Signalling, hell! They're shooting at us!'—I saw two bursts of flame before the word came to clear the bridge. I can't say how close how close they were to us as the radar had never been too dependable. It wasn't the night—but we were not hit. They never had a ping on us so it is assumed that they never had a fix on us."

One evening, lookout William "Radar" Hagendorn, having the night watch, was scanning the horizon during a stormy moonless night. The sea was running high and *Growler* was being tossed about. According to Radar, "One minute we would ride high on the crest of a wave and the next minute we would be deep in a valley. I trained my glasses forward and for an instant, I thought that I saw what could have been a ship's mast, but as quick as it disappeared. Using a technique that I learned in 'lookout school,' I soon got another glimpse and reported 'ship on the horizon!' which brought Skipper Schade to the bridge in an instant. However, even after looking through the higher power periscope plus giving a thorough search with the boat's radar, it was concluded that perhaps there was nothing there, that what I saw was an optical illusion!

William F. "Radar" Hagendorn

"In order to maintain my good reputation as a lookout, I kept an eye peeled in that sector and soon made the same report with the same results. No one else could see it! But Captain Schade wisely ordered a change of course toward my phantom sighting. My next report came shortly, but this time I reported 'signals on the starboard bow!'

"This time the officer of the deck shouted his order: 'Dive! Dive!' which signaled shells from enemy warship were being fired. They were coming from a Jap destroyer! Later it was concluded that when we and the Jap destroyer both rode the crest of a wave at the same time, it was possible to see over the horizon. When the story was told below deck, the conclusion was that I could see even better than radar! The nickname 'Radar' stuck!"

Hagendorn had enlisted in the Navy in 1940 and was on the USS *Long Island* (CVE-1) when the Japanese attacked Pearl Harbor. When his carrier was delivering aircraft to Guadalcanal in 1942, Hagendorn volunteered for the submarine service. He was assigned to the *Growler* and served on her for three war patrols the eighth through the tenth.

Hagendorn described the hardship of life on a submarine, saying, "One had to travel 10,000 miles at fifteen miles-per-hour in enemy-controlled waters without a major mechanical failure. A breakdown could mean death. The submarines carried no doctor, you had no days off, there was no sunshine. You breathed and exhaled air on the ship that was breathed by your mates until your head started aching from the lack of oxygen and the smell of diesel oil. There were no showers and when you came on shore people would back away from you.

"The pay was twenty-one dollars a month, with free room and board. But the courage and optimism of youth, these volunteers were committed to the red white and blue and this spirit did not waver."

During the typhoon being on the bridge was the "scariest and hairiest" moments in the life of Robert Link aboard the *Kangaroo Express*. *Growler* took rolls to port, and starboard of 60 degrees and at, one point, loading the bridge seawater pouring through the main air intake of the boat.

Link said, "At this point, we cleared the bridge and attempted to dive. It was several moments before the boat, started down and *Growler* assumed an up-angle while heading for deep water. Our depth gauge was off scale and when the boat was finally brought under control. Later, the after-torpedo room crew reported that we were over 400 feet before we stopped. We did attempt to cruise at periscope depth but we only found calm water at 200 feet. The swells run very deep during a typhoon.

"Departing from station on *Growler*'s eighth patrol running on the surface using periscope for fifth lookout destination Majuro Atoll for overhaul alongside tender *Perry*. Periscope lookout picked up target at several thousand yards.

"The *Kangaroo Express* dove and moved submerged toward target. It was determined that target could be sunk by deck guns. On deck there were three-and-one-half-inch guns forward, and on the bridge, two 20 mm guns. Link was told that he would be a trainer on the three-and-one-half inchers and crew mate Tagliapetra would be pointer.

Link said, "I had always been on the 20 mm in gunnery practice but for some reason a switch was made. No problem—I had been to torpedo and gunnery school. Seconds later we surfaced. The 20s were chattering and the gun crew was setting up the three and one half. We couldn't get the cover off the trainer's sight glasses so it was decided to sight through the web.

"By the time we moved in close for concentration, the 20s had pretty much demolished the cabin and whatever deck guns the patrol boat may have had. There was no noticeable return of fire. No one observed anyone on deck. They had either gone overboard or were hiding in the bilges. Our hits from bow to stern seemed initially not to do much damage except to inflict holes into the hull. In the end, an explosion in her engine room blew her out of the water. Strike another Empire gunboat.

Although no one on the deck was lost, it occurred to Link that submariners were on the surface a lot during battle. Link cited *Amberjack*'s loss of their pharmacist mate. The *Silversides* had also lost a crewman. And, of course, *Growler* had lost Gilmore, Williams and Kelley. All were the result of return fire. Link had not considered these possibilities during the surface battle. "Only after we had gone below and secured our battle stations, had I considered that at no time were we behind any kind of barrier. We were standing in the open at all times. Now if I am an enemy gunman, my aim is going to be at those shooting at me—either the pointer or the trainer."

2-5 April 1944:
>Very rough weather, but remained north of AMAMI O SHIMA, which still appears to be most likely spot for traffic.

8-9 April 1944:
>Patrolled to west of IO KITA JIMA.

10 April 1944:
>1127   CONTACT #14. Sighted through #1 periscope while on surface a small ship. Closed submerged. Battle Surfaced.
Ship identified as a 250T Naval Auxiliary, patrolling. Set him on fire and sank him by gunfire.

17 April 1944:
>1610   Rendezvoused with REMY, escort.

The *Kangaroo Express* travelled 2,810 miles from patrol area near southern tip of Japan to Majuro in the Marshall Islands.

Skipper Schade commented in his summary of the patrol that "rough weather caused as much worry as did the enemy, and probably prevented us from finding targets. Bridge personnel took a considerable beating. Twice the ventilation (and main induction) flooded with water entering the living spaces. Bunks and clothing were soaked."

A Japanese Naval Auxilliary vessel burns before sinking after being shelled by Growler, *April 1944.*

Admiral Lockwood's endorsement of *Growler*'s eighth war patrol stated that, despite extensive and effective antisubmarine activity in an area off Japan, *Growler*'s Skipper Schade and crew were congratulated for a successful patrol. *Growler* had earned a Combat Insignia Award.

Comments from the commander of Schade's Submarine Squadron Ten noted that *Growler* had much difficulty maintaining periscope depth due undoubtedly to heavy seas encountered throughout the patrol.

The lack of Nip shipping as evidenced by this and other recent patrols indicates:

    a. The more southern areas are "drying up."

    b. Japs are using more infrequent and larger convoys, or

    c. Shipping is being drawn closer to the so-called "Empire."

The commander of Division 102, Adm. Frank T. Watkins also noted that, *Growler*'s fifty-nine day eighth patrol in the Empire sea routes westward of Amami O Shima was effective under extreme conditions for inflicting damage upon the enemy. The offensive operations of *Growler* were hampered by exceedingly rough seas and foul weather accompanied by periods of poor visibility throughout the greater part, of the patrol. Despite these handicaps good area coverage was accomplished which resulted four worthy contacts, among which was a convoy headed for Bungo Suido.

In one incident *Growler* surfaced to challenge an enemy warship in a duel. After accomplishing a battle surface at an opening range of 2,500 yards, *Growler* manned her three-inch and 20 mm deck guns. Despite having to clear jams, the guns delivered fifteen hits as the range closed to 200 yards. The ship exploded and sank. There were no survivors.

Gung Ho!

Skipper Arnold Schade's last journey aboard his *Kangaroo Express* was to bring her into Majuro in the Marshall Islands on the 16th of April 1944 after completing her eighth war patrol. Schade had been aboard her at the beginning, in early 1942. He had been a part of her most daring actions. Schade must have had very strong emotions in having brought her safely to port on that spring day in 1944 to deliver her over to someone else. It had to have been a very painful separation.

There, Lt. Comdr. Thomas B. Oakley, Jr. USN, Naval Academy class of 1934, became *Growler*'s third, and tragically, last skipper. Schade recalled Oakley as "gung ho" in the best sense of that expression. Oakley was a brave aggressive commander. Schade was especially impressed by Oakley's first war patrol, *Growler*'s ninth, and has often expressed that fact. What a powerful unexpressed emotion that must have been in yielding his *Kangaroo Express,* even to someone he respected.

According to the Annapolis "Register of Alumni," T.B. Oakley, Jr. was graduated in 1934 and reached the rank of commander. His awards include the Navy Cross, Legion of Merit and the Bronze Star.

He was born 27 February 1912 in Staten Island, New York, the middle child of three children. He had an older sister, Betty, and a younger brother, John. At the time of death, he was thirty-two years, nine months and eight days. Only now do we realize just how young he really was.

Commander Ben had married the former Betty Breeden, who had a sister named Barbara, who in turn married Captain Warren Hall, also a submariner. As much as the girls wanted a double-wedding, it wasn't going to be, as the captain was still in the probationary period—that is, he hadn't been out of the academy for more than two years. Nevertheless, Commander Ben married Betty in 1939 which resulted in their firstborn son, Richard, in 1942. Oakley, already a submarine veteran, had made his first two runs as executive officer of the USS *Tinosa*. While aboard the *Tinosa*, he received a letter from his brother-in-law, Captain Hall, advising him to push for a split cubicle, because aboard the USS *Sunfish*, there had been a flash fire off the coast of Japan. Fortunately, although half of the wiring was fused, a jury-rig was made, enabling the boat to get back to port. Captain Warren had been chided for taking along diagrams of a split cubicle, but that is what saved the boat.

Lt. Comdr. Thomas B. "Ben" Oakley, Jr., Growler's *third and last skipper.*

Meanwhile, Oakely had gone aboard the old USS *Tarpon* as its new commanding officer on a special mission which would take him to the Marshall Islands. That run lasted only a short while, from early December of 1943 to late January of the following year, 1944. It was in Majuro, in the Marshall Islands, that Oakley took command of the *Growler* from Schade.

Growler, under Oakley's command, departed for Majuro on 14 May to take up her ninth patrol in the Marianas—Eastern Philippines—the Luzon area, where the first stages of the attack on the Marianas and the battle of the Philippine Sea were getting under way.

In his lengthy report on *Growler*'s ninth patrol, Oakley's report reads:

(A) <u>PROLOGUE</u>:

Arrived MA JURO on 16 April 1944, + 12 time, from eighth war patrol. Normal two week refit was conducted by U.S.S. SPERRY and Subdiv 102 relief crew. Officers and crew thoroughly enjoyed the new Rest and Recreation center. Lieutenant Commander Thomas B. Oakley, Jr. U.S.N. relieved Lieutenant Commander. Arnold F. Schade, U.S.N. of command on 23 April 1944. A seven day daylight training period was furnished, during which three Mk 14 exercise torpedoes were fired. The extra privilege of being the first boat to fire exercise torpedoes at this advanced base was greatly appreciated.

(B) <u>NARRATIVE</u>:

14 May 1944:

1400	Departed MA JURO with U.S.S. FAIN as escort. Using constant helm on a 95%, zig plan and making good 12 knots up the safety lane on two engines 80-90.
2315	Sighted searchlight beam.

18 May 1944:

Daily trim dive and surprise dive while blowing up. Conducted fire control problems. Exercised crew at general drills, battle stations and "Surprise Machine Gun Practice."

A handwritten note on *Growler*'s bulletin board dated 21 May 1944 said:

MEMORANDUM TO ALL HANDS

Tonight we will "arrive on station." Our area is known to be fruitful: it is also known to be well-protected by airplane searches. All hands must get on the ball, and stay there! You lookouts, sound men and radar watches remember that the safety of the ship and ourselves depends on your vigilance. For pete's sake keep alert. Also remember that the beer (prize for sighting or hearing or seeing a nip) on the radar is good (Ballentine or Acme and ice cold). Earn a bottle, we want to give it away. Dope will be published within a few days about qualification requirements. In the meantime start learning your own station thoroughly and the boat in general.

(Signed) R.K. Mason Jr., Executive officer.

This appears to be a reassurance to the crew that Schade's reassignment was appreciated and that the crew was in good hands. To be sure, the old hands would surely miss "Uncle Arnie" as he was affectionately called by his crew. Even today Admiral Schade beams as he acknowledges with pride that nickname.

24 May 1944:

0505	Submerged about 50 miles NE of SAIPAN. Bathythermo-

> graph indicated an isothermal to 175', a 2° thermocline to 195'
> and a 1° negative gradient to 285'. Commenced submerged
> patrol of shipping lanes to empire.

This all meant that there were hiding places in case of need. In certain thermal areas, a sub could hide undetected from enemy sounding devises.

Growler was to rendezvous with USS *Seahorse* and USS *Bang* to form a wolf pack in the Luzon area.

25 June 1944:

0120	Established communications with SEAHORSE. No sign of BANG. Since SEAHORSE has 20,000 gallons more fuel, it was decided that he would search toward FORMOSA while we remained near rendezvous.
2035	Surfaced. Headed for rendezvous.
2126	Established communication with SEAHORSE.
2154	Established communication with BANG. Lying to.
2235	BANG delivered message tube alongside. Received information relative to our future operations in "Convoy College."

28 June 1944:

0532	Have sufficient fuel to reach MIDWAY on one engine plus 10% reserve. Having informed BANG that we would remain in company for only three nights...went ahead on one engine 80-90.

In an area off Luzon, *Growler* continued to patrol, closing several large targets late in the evening of the 28th. A bright quarter moon about three hours high afforded very good visibility. *Growler* decided to end around target to eastward of target and to attack after moonset.

29 June 1944:

0100	Battle stations. Four engines on the screws, 80-90. Commenced approach using TBT bearings and radar ranges. Target zigging approximately every 12 minutes.
0133	Sighted small flickering white light and its position disclosed it to be a fourth escort. Could not see the outline of this escort whereas others are visible as long low, dark shapes. Range to target - 7,225 yards.
0208	Commenced attack. Wind force - 3, sky mostly overcast, dark with visibility fair.
0228	ATTACK I - Commenced firing 6 bow tubes set at 8 feet. Range to target 3,240 yards, gyro angle 1° right, total spread 3¼° closest escort 2,600 yards, shard on starboard bow. Would have set torpedoes for 6 feet had it not been for sea condition - 3. Theory: - to make certain of venting his tanks. At this time the target is about ½ the 7x50 binocular field in length. The escorts with the target are about half as long as it is. The light on the small escort is still on

	our port quarter. Upon completion of firing swung hard right to bring stern tubes on; steadied on 015 T.
0230	Observed the first hit. Heard two other detonations and then the explosion of the tanker. Now the Commanding Officer became concerned with the escort at range 1,700 yards. The TBT officer, Ensign Carr, USN who has witnessed 11 ships sink, observed at least 3 hits on the tanker. Sound reported seven detonations; while observers below report 4 explosions, a delay and than 4 more. The height of the column of black smoke and flame is estimated at 700' streamers of fire shot out in every direction resembling a "flower pot" of July 4th fame. The flash and blast of the target exploding were seen and felt by an officer stationed in the conning tower at the hatch. It is believed that the target was loaded with gasoline.
0234	Executive officer, radar officer and others observed the target's pip to disappear from the A scope and the PPI. When the smoke had lifted, a clear horizon was observed where the target had been. The target [*Katori Maru*] had sunk.
0239	After determining that the closest escort was not chasing (range 4,500 yards), the executive officer, radar officer and others observed but two pips on A scope and PPI. The third escort, which had been on either the target's port bow or quarter, had disappeared. Bridge observed two escorts astern. They were flashing small white lights. The fourth escort (with the light) was still far from the scene. One large escort had sunk. After much coaxing "Dame Fortune" and "Lady Luck" smiled at GROWLER.
0315	Sent results of attack on effective area frequency.

After two more weeks in the area *Growler* headed for an escort to Midway, arriving there on the 13th of July, then went on to Pearl Harbor.

In Skipper Oakley's first war patrol on *Growler*, six torpedoes were fired on the only attack of the mission. He was credited with sinking two ships, one, a large tanker and the other an escort, for a total of 10,600 tons. Admiral Lockwood congratulated *Growler* for a successful war patrol by presenting a Combat Insignia Award.

At another crucial period, Skipper Oakley took *Growler* to the Philippine Sea in the spring of 1944. The battle for the Marshalls was over, enabling *Growler* to depart from Majuro to help prepare the fleet to skip forth to the Marianas Islands in preparation for the battle of the Philippines.

It was a bold move by the Americans to leap from the Marshalls to the Marianas, bypassing the Carolines, not only for the distances involved but also for the exposure of Japanese strongholds on the flanks.

Photo courtesy of Bob Link

Pearl Harbor, July 1944. L. to r.: William Bergfield (lost), Daniel Bailko, William Waltz, and Lloyd Maness (lost).

Photo courtesy of Bob Link

Comdr. Thomas B. "Ben" Oakley at Pearl Harbor after the ninth run, July 1944.

The entire Growler *crew poses after the successful completion of the ninth war patrol. Pearl Harbor, July 1944.*

July 1944 in Pearl Harbor. L. to r. standing: Comdr. Ben Oakley, Plummer, Richard Mason, William Carr, Harry Messick. By flag: Norman Naylor, Jewett, Smith. Messick left Growler *in Perth; all others lost.*

Photo courtesy of Bob Link.

On leave in Pearl Harbor after the ninth war patrol, July 1944.
Albert Holsclaw is on left, Vercere, kneeling, sailor on right is unidentified.

Gilmore's Ghost

During this ninth war patrol aboard *Growler*, a spooky drama was taking place. According to Hagendorn, "It was referred to the ghost that haunted 'Arky' Mason. The mystery will almost certainly never be solved.

"Everyone has had the experience of laying something down, then reaching for it moments later only to find that it had mysteriously disappeared, even though you had never moved from that spot. It can be frustrating—it can lead you on the road to believing in ghosts. This is a story of not a single item disappearing but item after item, even though every precaution was taken to guard against it.

"Every submarine that was sent out to a war zone was issued bottles of brandy to be used for medicinal purposes during severe depth-charge attacks. Aboard the *Growler*, the executive officer was responsible for these small-sized bottles. Lt. Richard Mason Jr., the executive officer, was a very meticulous Southern gentleman. When the box of bottles was assigned to him were counted, it was always witnessed by a second officer before 'Arky' signed the receipt. He then put the precious cargo into a special metal locker in his cabin while recounting the bottles once more as he prudently stowed them. To further insure their safety, he clamped his own personal padlock on the door and the only key was chained around his neck. During any depth-charge attack, Mr. Mason would distribute an exact number of bottles, then relock the locker. When the attack ended, another count was taken and duly reported in a special log. During one such count, much to Mason's surprise, a number of bottles were missing.

" 'Hmmmmm,' mused Arky, 'the key has been around my neck and has never been off, even to take a shower.' The lock, even after a close inspection, showed no sign of tampering. Was it possible that the scrupulous lieutenant had miscounted? Impossible, so where were the missing bottles?

Mumbling to himself, he decided to take another count the following day when he had more time to think it over. But for safety, he changed the lock and glued an almost invisible hair over the keyhole, which would break when a key was inserted.

"Oh, how frustrating! However, the next day, in a calmer mood, another bottle count was taken. He first examined the hair, which was taken from his head. It was still in place, but again, after another count a bottle showed up missing. There was no logical explanation, unless there was a mysterious force, unknown to man, that had slipped aboard.

"Perhaps it was the ghost of Howard Gilmore, who had been killed in action the previous year, prowling the boat. It was common knowledge that Captain Gilmore was fond of a nip or two.

"But poor Arky Mason, lost when the *Growler* went on her final dive November 8, 1944, never did learn the secret of the shrinking supply of bottles. The answer evaded him because he knew that the locker was welded to the bulkhead and he was correct in assuming that the door had never been opened. But what Arky didn't know was that the Chief Petty Officer Bill Soczek's quarters was located adjacent to his, and because of some minor electrical problem, the panel box in the CPO's quarters was removed in order to complete the repair. By chance, the panel and Arky's locker were back to back. When Chief Soczek removed the panel, much to his surprise and delight, there appeared before his bulging eyes, row upon row of these little bottles all begging to be tasted.

"That electrical panel was always a source of trouble and, although it was dismantled a number of times, the repair never seemed hold up for very long," wrote Hagendorn.

Schade laughingly commented that on his watch the liquor was stored in his shower room. He recalled that Arky was a short man of about 140 pounds who, when in port, would order a case of beer to be brought to his hotel room each morning which he would consume during course of the day. The following is taken from the war patrol report of the ninth run:

PERSONNEL

The state of training of the officers and enlisted men of vessel is considered very good-excellent. Although several changes made were made in the vital routines by the new commanding officer, the officers and men responded admirably. The performance of duty of all hands under combat conditions was excellent. The tireless devotion to duty executive officer, Lieutenant R.K. Mason, Jr. USN, was an inspiration to all and a great source of reliance on the commanding officer. The officers and men could not have performed their duties so efficiently if they were not proud of themselves and their ship."   (Signed and posted)   Commander T. B. Oakley, Jr.

Ben's Busters

Growler's tenth run began on 11 August 1944, when she was directed from Pearl Harbor to Fremantle, Australia. From there Oakley formed a new wolf pack nicknamed Ben's Busters. In the company of *Sealion* and *Pampanito*, *Growler* headed for the Formosa Straits area. Aided greatly by reconnaissance and guidance from U.S. airplanes, Ben's Busters closed in for night surface action on 31 August. Their torpedoes plunged in to a Japanese force into chaos, with their own ships firing at each other in the dark. But there were no reported sinkings.

Almost two weeks later, on 12 September, the wolf pack sighted a second convoy and it closed for action. An account of this battle was provided by Capt. Harry Messick, then a lieutenant on board *Growler*:

Unknown to the wolf pack, the enemy convoy included three merchant ships which were being used as prison ships. The three prison ships had left Singapore jammed with 1,700 British and Australian prisoners of war, then stopped in the Philippines to take on 475 American prisoners. Months, even years of slave labor had reduced the men to speechless zombies. All suffered the common maladies of dysentery, malaria and jungle pestilence. The overcrowded holds where the men were kept were hellholes of filth and vermin.

In one incident, a couple of Japanese guards drafted a sergeant from a cabin where he had been interrogated to top side where he was severely beaten. A guard peeled back a tarpaulin from the prisoners' hold, which wretched forth a stench so nauseating that even the guards gagged, and threw the American into the hold, according to William Hagendorn in *Messick Special*. Meanwhile, Ben's Busters were ploughing through the Bashi Channel on the course of the three prison ships. "A jackpot," murmured *Growler*'s executive officer, Arkie Mason, to Comdr. Ben Oakley upon sighting the convoy. Radar showed sixteen enemy vessels. Six rode the flanks of the convoy and a seventh rode the spearhead. "That'll be the tin can," Oakley said, "and the ones on the flank are the escorts." He flashed his men a grin, "Okay, let's take them," according to Hagendorn. The following story is quoted with permission from the August 1988 edition of the *Kangaroo Express.*

"The 312-foot *Kangaroo Express* slipped through the murky water at ten knots," on the surface to 1,500 yards. Stand by bow tubes—fire one! Fire two! The Japanese frigate *Hirado's* lookout screamed a warning as he spotted the telltale torpedo's wake, but too late as two tons of torpedo with a 750-pound torpedo warhead exploded among stacked 5-inch shells in the frigate's magazine. The *Hitado* simply disintegrated.

"The three American submarines regrouped and quietly maneuvered into position for a second attack. At 0445 *Growler* fired a four-fish spread at the merchant ships and tankers. Two fish struck a freighter loaded with rice and crude rubber....two struck a pair of heavy oil tankers.

"Now it was Eli Reich's turn aboard the *Sealion.* As she broke surface, Eli bawled, 'make ready forward tubes.' Two fish slammed into the 3,500 ton *Nankai Maru* where more than 500 POWs broke into a frail cheer. The ship took on a 40-degree list hurling the trapped men into a pitiful heap. Sorting themselves out, they climbed the ladder to claw at the tarpaulin cover. The Japanese then opened one corner, not to assist the prisoners, but to hurl a hand grenade in on them! The men on the ladder, now partially dismembered, fell back into the slime and filth.

"The after hatch was opened and automatic rifle fire was turned on them at point blank range. They could only scream their protests. A wild-eyed Yank scrambled up the gruesomely slick ladder and grabbed the rifle barrel, held by a guard who then lost his balance and tumbled below among the crazed POWs. He was then promptly beaten, then stomped to death, drowning in the bloody, scummy filth.

"Reich's 21-inch torpedoes couldn't miss and two more crashed into the *Rakuyo Maru's* engine room and exploded. Half of her crew abandoned ship without orders. When the third torpedo hit, the POWs squirmed above decks, but were immediately transfixed in a crossfire of 25 caliber machine guns.

"Some 3,000 prisoners and Jap seamen thrashed in the salt water madly to escape the suction of the sinking ships, the still burning tankers bombarded the men with sizzling globs of oil while the 2,000-ton destroyer *Sikinami* crisscrossed the area to pick up their own men while sharpshooters sniped at the struggling Allied captives. The remnants of the convoy, now unescorted were hurrying prisoners at top speed over the horizon.

"Aboard the *Sikinami*, the captain called for full speed, then alerted his depth charge team. He was out for revenge. And *Growler* waited patiently.

"Oakley, alone on the bridge gave the order—'make all tubes ready' The range lessened and still Oakley held his fire. 'Range nine-oh-oh', then finally 'fire,' and the message of death sped towards the Jap destroyer at 50 knots an hour.

"Right full rudder, she swallowed four of 'em by god and she's coming for us like a mad bull!' The *Sikinami's* turbines were shattered but the momentum hurled her forward through the waves like a blazing battering ram, but Oakley's swift reaction avoided the ramming. The DD's magazine, then the boilers exploded and what was left sank like a stone. The adroit maneuvering by Oakley had taken *Growler* out of the enemy's way, but paint on her bridge was seared by the heat of the near miss of the passing destroyer."

Meanwhile *Pampanito's* skipper, Paul Summers, ordered his crew to help POWs in the water on board. At the same time he was fighting frigates. "The POWs were swimming and were under rifle fire but storm clouds began to bunch up and the Japs began to leave the area, not because of the approaching storm, but because the *Pampanito*, still surfaced, was ploughing toward the enemy ships with her 5 ¼-inch deck gun and 20 mm gun blazing. The combined Jap frigates converged on the lone U.S. sub but commander Summers dove the *Pampanito* and sent out a four-fish spread, hitting and sinking one of the attackers, but her sister frigates kicked the sub around with 600-pound depth charges. It was then that the *Sealion* and *Growler* arrived on the scene with guns trained on the enemy ships.

Growler stood off the two frigates with gun fire while the *Pampanito* and *Sealion* intensified rescue operations. Meanwhile COMSUBPAC had ordered the *Barb* and the *Queenfish* to the scene of rescue and battle.

The enemy frigates now gladly fled the scene leaving their own men to their watery fate, but now the race with the storm's fury began.

All night and the next day the big pick up went on. The submariners were shocked to see the ravaged bodies of the men being rescued, all due to brutality, dysentery, pellagra salt water sores, beri-beri scurvy and plain old starvation. Many were one hundred pounds underweight!

Growler had already left the scene, unaware of the plight of the POWs. Oakley and his crew did not learn of the rescue operation until they had returned to Australia.

The typhoon reached full fury before all of the POWs could be reached and many died just when that long-sought freedom was within their reach. Eli Reich stated that it pained him to leave the area, "but to stay was to risk all the lives and the sub itself. Just a little over two hundred men were returned to safety while the rest succumbed to the sea and the brutality of their captors."

When Ben's Busters returned to Fremantle on 26 September, they were credited with a total of six enemy ships sunk. *Growler* had sunk the destroyer *Shikinami* and the frigate *Mirado* while her companions had racked up two ships apiece. It was remarkable that the rescue operation was carried out despite rough seas caused by an approaching typhoon.

Capt. Harry J. Messick had a premonition: It was 20 October 1944, and the *Kangaroo Express* backs out of her slip in Fremantle, Australia to depart on her eleventh war patrol. Skipper Oakley is on the bridge guiding the submarine to her rendezvous with extinction. The old veteran-sub *Growler* had followed this exact same course ten times before and each time she had returned with scars which were the results of enemy action.

The first days of that final run were filled with the routine of drills, so that when the time came to face the enemy, the entire crew would work as one and with the precision of a finely tuned machine.

The previous run, which was the tenth, had been more than exciting, especially during the night surface attack on a Japanese convoy.

The *Growler* had waited just off the enemy's track, on the surface and under cover of darkness, allowing the IJN destroyer escort to cross her bow, which with her low silhouette made the sub almost invisible. All six of the *Growler*'s forward torpedo tubes were ready for immediate action.

The destroyer escort passed slowly by when suddenly she made contact with the sub, then came charging back with a zero angle. Captain Oakley immediately cleared the bridge, but he himself remained there alone.

The destroyer was bearing down at full speed, but Oakley coolly ordered the "torpedo data computer" setup to be changed from the convoy to the destroyer and gave constant target-bearing transmitter readings for a down the throat shot, on the surface! The confident Jap thundered in for the kill, but, the order from Oakley, "Fire one, fire two," and so forth was given until the full load of six torpedoes were fired. He then ordered, "Hard left rudder, all ahead flank." The crew below responded instantaneously as the *Growler*'s screws bit into the black waters.

With the sub going at hard left and the Japanese destroyer coming hard right to ram, she steered right into the path of those oncoming deadly fish. One, maybe two, fish slammed into the thin-skinned destroyer, stopping her dead, but the momentum put *Growler* alongside the destroyer, according to the *Kangaroo Express.*

The plotting officer, Lt. Harry Messick, came up to the bridge just in time to see the destroyer alongside the *Growler*, afire and heeled over, with the Japanese sailors in their white uniforms, climbing over the gun turrets. Tracer bullets crisscrossed the *Growler*'s bridge but Oakley remained topside until the boat was able to clear the immediate area. Later it was discovered that the paint on *Growler*'s bridge was blistered from the intense heat from the burning IJN *Hitado*. "Scratch one Jap man-o-war," said Messick.

Upon clearing the area, the torpedomen worked with amazing speed reloading those six empty torpedo tubes. At daybreak a deadly *Fubuki*-class destroyer was sighted. The boat immediately submerged and the words "battle stations" were passed silently throughout the boat. But the *Growler* had been spotted and the destroyer moved fast, hoping to avenge the loss of the other destroyer only hours before. She bore in with a zero angle on the bow which made it possible for the *Growler* to use the same tactic on the destroyer escort. Six torpedoes were loosed on the hapless destroyer and they sped down the track for another-down-the-throat shot. Terrific explosions were heard and felt aboard the submarine and she came up for a look with the 'scope. The IJN *Shikinami* had simply disappeared! The *Growler* surfaced and headed for Australia. Scratch another man-o-war!

While heading back, the masts of three destroyers were sighted. They no doubt were headed for the area which the *Growler* had just vacated. Messick had the watch and, when the three destroyers were sighted, he reversed course and called Oakley to the bridge.

However, the *Growler* had only a single torpedo remaining, and so was forced to submerge, letting those three "freight trains" rumble on by while *Growler* listened barely a hundred feet away!

Notice to all hands: 15 September 1944

1. Fremantle refit

2. We are going by way of Sulu and Celebes seas, may take three weeks.

3. All land bordering our route is in enemy hands. Enemy has control of air.

4. There is much shallow and dangerous water on the route. There will be many patrol boats and sampans. Be prepared to man any gun at any time.

5. In my opinion and in the opinion of the officers, the patrol is just beginning!!

6. All hands stand your most alert watch.

Thank you and good luck.   (signed) T. B. Oakley

Of course that was during the tenth run and now the boat was again out to sea on her eleventh, where Messick was on watch in the conning tower. Suddenly, without any warning, an explosion rocked the boat coming from somewhere below. Immediately, the boat took on an extreme angle and headed for the bottom like a rock. Water bubbled up from the control room, filling the conning tower where Messick stood, transfixed! The water swept him off his feet and in order to preserve his life as long as possible, he began to swim upward to look for a pocket of air that would be trapped in the after part of the compartment. He was in a desperate situation, as he began treading water and suddenly knew he was doomed!

But wait—while treading water desperately he was no longer in the conning tower, but was in his bunk located in the forward battery, and his tired legs were bicycling in desperation! The eleventh run hadn't started yet, it was just a dream. The boat was still a few days out of Fremantle where the tenth run would come to an end.

Harry Messick, never a man to put any belief in dreams or a peek into the future type of nonsense, just shrugged it off as a bad dream, which was the result of the high action during the last few days. The practical lieutenant was in charge again! Messick's dream, as repeated by Hagendorn, was terribly realistic.

According to the *Kangaroo Express*, "The next night after completing his watch, Messick crawled into his bunk for a much-needed rest. The same dream returned and for the second time he awoke while desperately

Photo courtesy of Bob Link.

Growler *crew members, (l. to r.) Robert Manske, William Booker and Ralph Hope pose with the flag in Perth, Australia, in October 1944, shortly before* Growler *left on her eleventh and last run.*

bicycling in the corner of his bunk gasping for that pocket of trapped air in the coming tower. The practical lieutenant was now doing some deep thinking; was this just a warning from the other side because perhaps it wasn't his time to go as yet? Was he following a predestined path the same as the salmon follows when it returns to its place of birth to spawn?"

During the refit of the *Growler* in Fremantle, Harry Messick received orders to report for new construction aboard the USS *Entemedor,* but his detachment papers didn't arrive until barely a half hour before *Growler's* departure for her fatal eleventh run! What caused the delay on the transfer? His relief was replaced at his own request by still another officer who was perhaps destined to be aboard for that final run.

Milton Weymouth, like Messick, left *Growler* just before her last run. During *Growler's* last reunion in Texas, one of the survivors, Art Ullrich, remarked to *Kangaroo Express* editor Hagendorn, that Milton was one of *Growler's* crew who stood out from the crowd and wondered why one of the most outstanding was never written up in the *Kangaroo Express*.

With Ben Oakley's naval days of glory fading into history, we can only honor the men of the *Growler* with our inadequate words. Although Oakley was an aggressive commanding officer, he was a man of compassion, which was shown on *Growler's* ninth patrol while heading back to base.

Messick recalled that "A handful of Japanese soldiers were spotted floating on a large wooden raft on the vast pacific ocean. We pulled alongside and offered to take them aboard but they refused! The general thought was that if they could survive, perhaps they would be able to one day return and kill an American. But Captain Oakley, who could have the raft sunk or destroy their supplies, simply said, let them be, they are miserable enough. We sailed in an easterly direction to Pearl Harbor.

"From that brief encounter we knew that Ben Oakley, who wanted desperately to sink Japanese ships, wouldn't step beyond the rules of fairness. His sportsmanship wouldn't allow him to take unfair advantage, even in war. He exemplifies what a true naval officer should be and sets a fine example for others to follow by his high personal standards learned at the U.S. Naval Academy. How sad that he never saw his son grow to manhood, nor to enjoy the liberty that he fought and died for."

After that nightmarish tenth patrol, Harry Messick was ordered to New London to put the submarine USS *Entemedor* in commission as executive officer. Thus, as Trumbull says "of the four of us who joined *Kangaroo Express* in April 1943, Mason, myself, Naylor and Messick, Messick and myself went onto other subs while Mason and Naylor went down with the *Growler.*"

Last Run

Out of Fremantle on 28 October 1944 under the command of Skipper T. B. Oakley, Jr., *Growler* led a wolf pack with *Hake* and *Hardhead*. The pack's destination was an area off southwest Luzon, where they were to join the SUBSOWESPAC forces blocking the approaches to Manila and Mindoro. Veteran of the Aleutian struggle and the Solomon-Bismark fighting, *Growler* will be remembered as the submarine that rammed an enemy warship on the road to Rabaul.

Growler disappeared on its eleventh war patrol on 8 November 1944 with a loss of all eighty-six on board. Submarines *Growler*, *Hake* and *Hardhead* were operating together, out of Fremantle to west of the Philippine group, as a coordinated search and attack wolf pack. On 7 November, *Growler* reported having made temporary repairs to her SJ radar which

Photo courtesy of Bob Link

*Growler's battle flag flies proudly from her conning tower
shortly before embarking on her final run.*

made it usable, but that she urgently needed spare parts for it. A rendezvous was scheduled with *Bream* for the purpose of delivering parts.

In the early morning hours of 8 November, *Growler*, then in 13 N, 119 E degrees, made SJ radar contact on an enemy target group, and radioed it to *Hardhead*. Commander Oakley directed *Hardhead* to track and attack from the convoy's port bow. Shortly thereafter, *Hardhead* made contact with both the target group and *Growler*. After about an hour had passed, *Hake* heard two distant explosions of undetermined character, which sounded like a torpedo. At the same time, the targets zigged away from *Growler*. Shortly after, *Hardhead* heard three distant depth charges explode. The order to attack was the last communications ever received from *Growler*.

A little over an hour after these explosions, *Hardhead* attacked the target from the port bow, obtained three of four hits, and *Hake* saw a tanker sink. *Hardhead* was subjected to a severe counterattack from which it emerged undamaged, while *Hake* was worked over thoroughly later in the morning. All attempts to contact *Growler* after this attack were unsuccessful and she has never been seen or heard from since. The rendezvous with *Bream*, for the delivery of SJ spare parts, was not accomplished. Since *Growler* had tracked the targets by radar for at least an hour, it appears that her temporary SJ repairs must have been satisfactory.

Although Japanese records mention no antisubmarine attacks at this time and place, it is evident that depth charges were dropped in the vicinity of *Growler*, but in the absence of more conclusive evidence the cause of her loss must be described as unknown. The Japanese admitted that a tanker was sunk that night which checks with *Hardhead's* sinking. *Hardhead* was heavily depth-charged following her own attack and later that morning *Hake* was expertly worked over presumably by the same escorts. This leads to the belief that if *Growler* was sunk by depth charges it was at the hands of a skillful antisubmarine group.

The explosion described by *Hardhead* as "possibly a torpedo" may have been a depth charge or a torpedo explosion. It is unlikely that a torpedo hit was made on the convoy at this time because if the tanker had been hit, she probably would either have burst into flame, as she was subsequently when hit by *Hardhead*, or slowed down hit, in the engine room. She did neither, nor was there any evidence that any of the three escort's were hit. However, since only three subsequent explosions were heard by *Hake*, and a number of depth charges generally are dropped in an accurate persistent, antisubmarine attack, a number of possibilities exist as to *Growler*'s end.

She could have been sunk as a result of a premature or circular run of her own torpedo, and the three depth charges heard by *Hake* may have

Postal Telegraph

C1 85 GOVT=WASHINGTON DC 2 142A
MR & MRS VINCENT F BERGFELD=
2821 MOULTRIE AVE MATTOON ILL=

1944 DEC 2 AM 7 54

THE NAVY DEPARTMENT DEEPLY REGRETS TO INFORM YOU THAT YOUR
SON, WILLIAM VINCENT BERGFELD, ELECTRICIANS MATE FIRST
CLASS, USN IS MISSING FOLLOWING ACTION WHILE IN THE SERVICE
OF HIS COUNTRY. THE DEPARTMENT APPRECIATES YOUR GREAT
ANXIETY BUT DETAILS NOT NOW AVAILABLE AND DELAY IN RECEIPT
THEREOF MUST NECESSARILY BE EXPECTED. TO PREVENT POSSIBLE
AID TO OUR ENEMIES AND TO SAFEGUARD THE LIVES OF OTHER
PERSONNEL PLEASE DO NOT DIVULGE THE NAME OF HIS SHIP OR
STATION OR DISCUSS PUBLICLY THE FACT THAT HE IS MISSING=
VICE ADMIRAL RANDALL JACOBS
THE CHIEF OF NAVAL PERSONNEL.

MEMORIAL DAY IS MAY 26th, FLY THE AMERICAN FLAG....

This telegram was received by Mrs. Bergfeld, and sent by Bill's brother, Don Bergfeld. I am reproducing it as a reminder of the sacrifices that were made not only by the 3,505 men who are on "Eternal Patrol!" but the many lives that were affected and deeply touched by their personal loss.

Time has softened the hurt but it can never erase the tragedy that each family had to bear in silence. The parents, brothers, sisters, wives and children had to wait a full year before they found out with certainty that the U S S Growler had no survivors.

Before very long it again will be Memorial Day, and many people attend the many observances throughout the land, but it has become a festive day with picnics and merriment emphasized, rather than the emphasis on recall of those who gave their lives in a time when survival of our country was at stake.

This year let every submariner, and especially every man from the Growler impress upon the younger generation, the importance of this day. Fly the colors proudly from sunrise to sunset.....

been only a token by the escort. Although there was a quarter moon, the night was somewhat, misty, and she may have made the approach at radar depth. If so, she could have been rammed, thus making it unnecessary for the escort, to drop many depth charges. She could have been caught, at either radar or periscope depth and the antisubmarine group, evidently an effective one, might, have verified the results of their attack immediately. An escort could have hit, her with a torpedo and only dropped a few depth charges to insure a kill.

Growler War Patrols

#	Date	Departing	Days	Skipper	Patrol Area
	2/11/41	Growler launched—Electric Boat Co. Groton, Ct.			
	20/3/42	Commissioned—Howard W. Gilmore, commanding			
	6/6/42	Pearl Harbor	15	H.W. Gilmore	Midway
1st	24/6/42	Pearl Harbor	27	H.W. Gilmore	Kiska, Alaska
2nd	5/8/42	Pearl Harbor	49	H.W. Gilmore	Formosa
3rd	22/10/42	Pearl Harbor	49	H.W. Gilmore	Truk
4th	1/1/43	Brisbane	48	H.W. Gilmore	Rabaul
	7/2/43	Killed in action: Skipper Gilmore, Ensign William W. Williams and F3c Wilbert F. Kelley 3°34'S 151°09'E, (NW of Kavieng, New Ireland)			
5th	13/5/43	Brisbane	48	A.F. Schade	Mussau Island
6th	21/7/43	Brisbane	53	A.F. Schade	Hermit Islands
7th	9/1043	Brisbane	35	A.F. Schade	New Ireland
	15/11/43	Growler ordered to extensive repairs			Hunters Point
8th	21/2/44	Pearl Harbor	55	A.F. Schade	Amami O Shima
9th	14/5/44	Majuro	64	T.B. Oakley, Jr.	Marianas-Luzon
10th	11/8/44	Pearl Harbor	45	T.B. Oakley, Jr.	Luzon-Formosa
11th	15/10/44	Fremantle	*	T.B. Oakley, Jr.	Mindoro
*	8/11/44 Growler was lost with all hands: 13N 119E off Mamburao.				

In any event, sinking by her own torpedoes is but a slight possibility. It is doubtful whether a report by this convoy would help to decide this question. In other cases, such as *Tullibee* and *Tang*, where survivors' statements leave little doubt that destruction was by their own torpedoes, the Japanese who picked up survivors claimed to have sunk the submarines.

All efforts to contact *Growler* for the next three days proved futile, and the gallant submarine was listed as lost in action against the enemy, cause

Distances

From:	To:	Nautical miles (rounded)*
Groton	Panama	2,300
Panama	Pearl Harbor	4,700
Pearl Harbor	Midway	1,300
	Rabaul	3,500
	San Francisco	2,100
	Tokyo	3,400
Midway	Kiska	1,500
	Formosa	3,100
	Tokyo	2,200
	Truk	1,800
Brisbane	Rabaul	2,000
	Bismark	2,000
	Pearl Harbor	4,200
Fremantle	Celebes	2,800
	Formosa	4,000
13 N 119 E	Mindoro	3,500

*one nautical mile equals 1.150779 statute miles.
 One degree of latitude at the equator equals about 69 statute miles.

unknown. Admiral Schade, to this day, believes *Growler* was hit and destroyed by her own torpedo(es).

Growler received eight Battle Stars for her service in World War II. During her ten reported patrols *Kangaroo Express* sank seventeen ships, totalling 74,900 tons, and severely damaged seven with 34,100 tons, a total of 109,000 tons of enemy shipping either sunk or out of commission.

Part 3

Finale

1944–1945

Mystery

Japanese submarines of the I-class were large. Almost two thousand tons, 350-feet long with a cruising radius of 16,000 miles, they could have delivered major damage to the United States, particularly to the Panama Canal where American warships traversed to the Pacific theater of war. The mystery is why?

Certainly, they had the range. A round trip from Japan to Panama is roughly 10,000 miles. They had an airplane on board and twelve torpedoes. A number of these subs could have closed the Canal down forcing U.S. warships to take a much longer route around the South America Cape Horn. Why?

Perhaps the answer lay with the Japanese High Command. Tojo was an army general and the army controlled the Navy. The Japanese submarine force did not enjoy the same confidence that the United States.

Admiral Schade says that the Japanese had good submarines and equipment only they just didn't know how to deploy them as did the United States. They were used more for logistic purposes rather than combat.

The Japanese submarines did have a few successes. While the Japanese media proclaimed it differently, the first wasn't really a success. Rather, it was a wake up call to United States coastal defenses.

More than two months after the sneak attack Pearl Harbor the Japanese submarine I-17, commanded by a former tanker crewman familiar with the area, Captain Nishimo, carrying a crew of eighty-five men, a small airplane, twelve torpedoes and a five-inch deck gun entered the Santa Barbara Channel. A nine-man gun crew opened fire on Ellwood's Richfield Oil Refineries. Most shells were duds. It was the first time since the war of 1812 that an enemy had fired on American shores.

Although the damage from the shelling was estimated at $500, radio Tokyo broadcast: "The U.S. War department officially announced that Santa Barbara, California, was devastated by enemy bombardment by a Japanese submarine. The attack occurred near the city of Ellwood and all military establishments were shelled and wrecked.

The United States Navy, whose ships are responsible for the protection of coastal areas, is not publicizing the damage however, for fear of the impact on the minds of the public. The United States Navy failed to protect its people because the fleet lies on the bottom of Pearl Harbor after the attack by Japan on 8 December [their time].

The other enemy attack on American soil was in the area of Fort Stevens in Oregon. Warrant flying officer Nobuo Fujita, a submarine-based pilot, took off from the I-25 and bombed the forests in an effort to cause fires. A heavy rain at the time resulted in the failure of his mission.

Admiral Schade believes that Japan's ineffective use of her submarines was more due to ignorance than to their capabilities. Top leadership did not appreciate the submarine's capabilities. Nor did it understand how to deploy them. They paid for that lapse dearly.

The Japanese submarine was larger, faster, and carried torpedoes that were very good—their "Long Lance"—packing a thousand pounds of explosives, could travel thirteen miles at a mile a minute without a telltale wake, exploding upon contact.

But their performances at Pearl Harbor and the West Coast of the United States relegated them to second-class status. During the late 1942 battle for Guadalcanal their submarines were used to deliver supplies and equipment. So instead of being a strategic weapon they had a logistical role.

Although they had sunk aircraft carriers *Yorktown* (already dead in the water and badly damaged), the *Wasp*, the cruiser *Indianapolis*, and the destroyer *O'Brien*, they were generally unproductive. Had the Japanese submarine been used as effectively as the American submarines the outcome of World War II may have been prolonged.

Strike Three!

The Japanese have long been baseball fans. This is a *Kangaroo Express* tale of sports remembered by Levon Hammond. "It occurred in 1945 while I was assigned to the USS *Club* where we were given rest and recreation leave in the Philippine Islands. A baseball game was in progress over at Rizal Stadium, and being interested in sports, I went over to watch. Also watching were some Japanese prisoners of war, who should have been clearing away some war damage but their attention was more on the game.

"Before Manila was occupied, Rizal Stadium was a large major league field, and because of its immensity, it was extremely hard to hit a home run, especially through center field. Of course it had been done by some of the professional players and each time one had succeeded in hitting a home run, the man's name was painted on the spot where the ball had passed over.

"Although the Japanese had played the game all during the occupation, not a single man could add his name to the existing 'Honor Roll' on the fence. There were only four names which were left unmolested during the war years out of respect. After the game I walked over to inspect the "Honor Roll" and it was quite obvious that the names had been painted years ago. As I walked along the fence, I reached deep center field, where it was the longest distance from home base and the most difficult point a homer.

"As I read the single name that had been painted long before the war and although time had taken its toll on the paint, the name stood out clear in the afternoon sun: Tex Forrest USN. Tex Forrest was a very large man and very strong. He was a machinist mate 1/c who had served aboard the *Growler*."

Arnie and the Pirates

After Admiral Lockwood resolved the torpedo problem at the end of September 1943, the Pacific Submarine Fleet's efficiency improved dramatically. Submarines in 1944 sank 529 merchant ships totaling 2.3 million tons, almost half of the war's total to date. Supplies of the Japanese war machine was dramatically curtailed.

The toll on Japanese warships was the same in 1944 with the sinking of a battleship, seven aircraft carriers, two heavy cruisers, seven light cruisers, thirty destroyers, and last, but not least, seven submarines. So by the end of 1944 the Japanese navy was no longer a threat.

The new fleet boat USS *Bugara* was commissioned 15 November 1944 with Arnold Schade as her skipper. She made three war patrols in the waning days of the war. The first was in February 1945 departing from Pearl Harbor for fifty-four days and returning to Fremantle, where Rear Admiral Christie was in command. Brisbane had all but closed down in late 1944 and Rear Admiral Fife had returned to Washington by December of 1944.

Bugara's second patrol, out of Fremantle in April to the South China Sea lasted forty days. Skipper Schade's final war patrol was in July of 1945 out of Fremantle for the South China Sea, lasting thirty-four days. Someone called it a "*Maru* Mop-up."

Getting back into action in early 1945, Schade found few challenges. The silent service had done such a good job that there was not much left. In fact they last major battle that the U.S. submarines had engaged in was the Battle of the Leyte Gulf in late October 1944.

But surface gun actions kept submarine patrols in action and significant tonnages were downed in these forays. Schade spent the rest of the war hunting down "Sea Trucks." Sea trucks were supply ships of about a thousand tons displacement transporting much-needed goods in the Gulf of Siam between Singapore and Japan. Patrolling in the Gulf of Siam, Schade, sent a record fifty-seven of these craft to the bottom.

Someone has compared these actions to Milton Caniff's "Terry and the Pirates." Admiral Schade chuckles and provides some stories to endorse this analogy.

All except two of these craft were boarded and their native crews were put safely ashore with their personal belongings and then blown out of the water.

In one encounter Schade came across a Japanese ship manned by a Chinese crew under attack by dangerous Malay pirates. *Bugara* rescued the Chinese, sank the ship and did the pirates in.

In another incident, Schade captured a ship which had non-Japanese Asian hands. One, a Chinese who had been an English professor in Singapore before the war, advised Skipper Schade that he was in command and that all Japanese officers on board were secured in the forecastle. While it has never been determined how the Chinese got the nickname "Charlie Chan," he volunteered to be Schade's interpreter. As he spoke Japanese as well, Schade wisely put Charlie into an American sailor's uniform as part of the crew. When a sea truck was stopped, the adopted interpreter told the Japanese skipper to surrender his logs, maps and other records, abandon ship, and then Skipper Schade sent the enemy vessel to the bottom.

Returning to port in Brisbane, Skipper Schade had difficulties in bringing in the Chinaman as all Asians were barred from entry into Australia during the war. But Schade was eventually successful in obtaining special dispensation. Charlie remained with *Bugara* through the duration of the war. He stayed on board until *Bugara*'s return to the United States when he was turned over to the Chinese Embassy. Charlie was never heard of again.

Epilogue

In his memoirs, Fleet Admiral Chester Nimitz compared submariners of early World War II to those brave young fliers in the first days of the European war, who fought the Battle of Britain against all odds, giving the Allies time to prepare for the great war. And so it was as submarines were the first to bring the war to the enemy Empire paying dearly for disrupting its supply routes giving the United States the time it desperately needed to counter the Japanese threat.

Think about it! The *Growler*, in its thousand days traveled a one hundred thousand miles using a million gallons of fuel. About three hundred men served aboard her during World War II. *Growler* sank or damaged twenty-four ships for a total tonnage of one hundred thousand tons expending over one hundred torpedoes in the process. In the end, she went down with the loss of all eighty-six men on board. The epic of Skipper Schade, *Growler*, and her crew is truly one of great heroes.

The USS *Growler* Sailing (Muster) List, dated 20 March 1942, included sixty-nine members plus two more who were picked up along the way for her first run. At this writing, the following men who commissioned the Growler are still alive:

Schade, Arnold F. Lt.	Holmes, Joseph J. AS
Currie, John P. Lt. j.g.	Kight, Delbert Tm2c
Bialko, Daniel M. F3c	Maske, Robert F. NM2c
Creeger, Harold L. S1c	McFall, Louis R. RM1c
Davis, William R. TM3c	Pugh, Jake
Gordon, Allan H. F1c	Schultz, Charles J. S2c
Grossman, David A. TM1c	Soczek, William FC2c
Hammond, Levon S1c	Stephans, Houston
Hilsabeck, Delbert B. TM3c	Triplette, Howard, EM3c

Ullrich, Arthur K. EM2c   Weymouth, Milton W. NM2c
Wagner, William QM1c

As I write this on Independence Day 1997, I am thinking about the above listed men who made *Growler*'s spectacular first war patrol fifty-five years ago.

After the war *Kangaroo Express* surviving veterans all went their separate ways, but each year, on 8 November, those who are able gather to honor those who are gone.

A Vow to Perpetuate Their Memory

It was the eighth of November, during the war,

the *Growler* disappeared, in the year forty-four.

But the crew is still alive, and the boat is like new,

because they live forever, in the hearts of us few.

Arnold F. Schade had participated in eleven War Patrols in the Pacific against Imperial Japan's naval forces: eight in the "USS *Growler*," and three in the USS *Bugara*. He served as the executive officer in the *Growler*'s first four war patrols and then took over as her skipper on the night of 7 February 1943, when Comdr. Howard W. Gilmore was killed in action.

The highlight of his career was the people with whom he served. In recalling the emotion of leaving the *Growler* for the last time, Schade said, "I was leaving with the last of the crew that had been with me through all of this. A lot of them had made numerous patrols with the *Growler*. By numerous, I mean three or four. That's a half a year's clip. They were upset. They were very loyal and determined to keep the memory of the *Growler* alive, which they are today. We meet every year for a reunion, and its a very emotional meeting when we get together. They were loyal, and I was trying to protect them all."

Lieutenant Commander Schade was awarded the Navy Cross for extraordinary heroism, while serving in the *Growler* during the first four war patrols in hostile waters. A Silver Star medal was awarded him for extremely valiant and intrepid conduct as executive officer and assistant approach officer of the *Growler* during an aggressive submarine war patrol in alien waters. He was awarded a Bronze Star medal with combat V for the *Growler*s Fifth War Patrol in enemy Japanese-controlled waters from 12 May to 30 June 1943. In early 1944 Commander Schade returned to the Pacific War as skipper of the newly commissioned *Bugara* for three war patrols in Japanese-controlled waters. For meritorious achievements in the *Bugara*, on her third war patrol, he was awarded a Gold Star medal with combat V in lieu of a second Bronze Star.

Schade's services from 1946 through 1966 included: executive officer and operations officer, administrative command, Mare Island; executive officer of the tender USS *Bushnell*; operations officer of the USS *McKinley*: of COMSUBDIV 12, during nuclear testing at Eniwetok in the early 1950s when the first hydrogen bomb was detonated at the Bikini Atoll in 1954; Armed Forces Staff College, Norfolk, Virginia; staff of Commander in Chief Naval Forces, Eastern Atlantic and Mediterranean; SUBGRU One, Mare Island, Pacific Reserve Fleet; National War College, Washington D.C.; USS *Seminole*; staff of National War College; commander SUBRON Six; Harvard University Fellowship with mentors Henry Kissinger and Brezshinski; head of Navy Plans Branch in the Office of Naval Operations; director, Political-Military Policy Division, in the Office of Chief of Naval Operations: Commander of Middle East Force headquartered in Manama, Bahrain; awarded the Legion of Merit; deputy Commander in Chief, USN Forces in Europe and chief of staff to the chief USN Forces; assistant chief of Naval Operations (plans and policy), Navy Department.

During his tenure as director, Politico-Military Policy Division and Branch of Chief of Naval Operations, Rear Admiral Schade set up a cot in the Pentagon at the time of the Cuban missile crisis to monitor the Soviet Union's attempt to supply Cuba with offensive missile sites which could launch nuclear warheads on American targets.

The United States response was to order a naval "quarantine" on the 22nd of October 1962. Admiral Schade provided the White House, often directly to President John F. Kennedy, daily briefings on the status of our blockade against the Soviet action.

In the end the Soviet Union backed down. No one better than Schade really knew how close to World War III the United States was.

In 1966 Schade was promoted to vice admiral and commander Atlantic Submarine Forces which employed a highly effective nuclear force capable of striking an enemy threat anywhere in the world.

The USS *Scorpion* was one such submarine. During exercises in the Atlantic she disappeared on the 27 May 1968. At the time it was the height of the Cold War and rumors abounded, ranging from sabotage by some unknown group, to a confrontation with a Soviet nuclear submarine.

The sub was eventually located on the 31st of October 1968, about 400 miles southwest of the Azores at a depth of 10,000 feet. Because of the immense pressure almost two miles down, the *Scorpion* had imploded with the loss of all hands.

Admiral Schade spent a great deal of his time investigating the cause of the tragedy. While the official Board of Enquiry was inconclusive, Schade believes that the *Scorpion* sank because of mechanical failure in its exhaust system. In the early morning odorless fumes seeped throughout the boat and the crew drifted off into unconsciousness and the *Scorpion* sank to such a deep depth that it simply imploded from the intense pressure.

Prior to retiring after forty-two years of active Navy service, Admiral Schade had been assigned, in addition, to Commander Eastern Sea Frontier; and, Commander Third Naval District; chairman of the Military Staff Command—United Nations. He reported directly to the Security Council which is the United Nations powerhouse. Admiral Schade says that many of the world's problems could be solved. But he regrets the loss of its effectiveness in recent history. Schade laments, "We could work things out then."

In 1971, Arnold Frederic Schade retired to Port Charlotte, Florida, with his wife, Becky. Even in retirement he became active in civic affairs. In 1972 he was chairman of the Charlotte County Development Authority (which oversees the Charlotte County Airport); 1973 chairman of the Charlotte County Commission and, in 1981 chairman of the Board of Trustees of Cultural Center Adult Education Association (Port Charlotte Cultural Center).

Arnie, as his friends call him, and Becky are regularly visited by their progeny of four daughters, seventeen grandchildren and twenty-two great grandchildren which total forty-three—about half the number for his World War II fleet boat. Now that's a force to be reckoned with.

The *Growler* tragedy is commemorated each year by the surviving crews of the *Growler*. On the 8th of November 1988 Schade's home Kiwanis Club in Port Charlotte, Florida, had the honor of hosting the commemorative reunion at their meeting place in the American Legion Post 110, where Schade is also a distinguished member. In all, 219 men served on the *Growler* from the time that it was commissioned and until it was lost. There still were forty men alive. Twenty were present at the reunion and memorial service.

Memories from Other Crew Members

At war's end, **Charles Trumbull** was aboard the USS *Cabezon* in Saipan, preparing for her second war patrol. He had left *Growler* in July 1944, after five runs, to return to the United States to commission the new fleet boat as executive officer on 30 December 1944. *Cabezon,* then had one war patrol

Trumbull said that instead of heading back to the United states, she as well as twelve other submarines were ordered to Subic Bay, the Philippines, where a new squadron was being formed. "This was the brainchild of Rear Adm. James Fife, and there we stayed for five months.

"The officers entertained themselves mainly at a recreation area consisting of a volleyball court, a softball diamond, a large swimming hole formed by a dammed creek, and an officer's club nearby. Enlisted men had similar facilities.

Photo courtesy of Bob Link

"Uncle Arnie" Schade, Charles Trumbull and Harry Messick
at the 1994 Growler reunion.

"Each of the eight boats would take turns going to Manila for rest and recreation. As a group, the eight made a tour around Luzon, visiting the Lingayen Bay, Casiguran Bay and the town of Legaspi on the southeast tip of Luzon where the spectacular Mayon volcano is located. On an earlier trip we all went on to Itu Aba, an island on Tizzard Bank, a part of what is known as 'The Dangerous Grounds' in the South China Sea. This island had been occupied by the Japanese and we were to see if any of them were still there. None were!

"All in all, we had a worthwhile and enjoyable time while in Subic, but we would all have rather been back in the USA," said Trumbull.

He said there were "many interesting facets of World War II submarine war patrols that do not get mentioned in the patrol reports which, of course, are official documents, not given to relating bits of human interest items."

With many, many months, nights and days, spent cruising the oceans at all latitudes, one observes many aspects of the life within those oceans.

Trumbull related one such experience. He was on an extended, three-month "simulated war patrol" from December 1946 to March 1947, cruising from Pearl to Samoa to Kapingamarangi to Truk to Guam to Okinawa to Yokuska and back to Pearl via Midway.

Hagendorn, Ullrich and Feit in Chicago, 1984.

"A situation that would not necessarily have occurred during wartime, Skipper Otis Cole would often stop mid-ocean and hold a swim call. With the submarine stopped dead in the water, and with a sharpshooter in the periscope shears and a man or two on the bridge with whistles in case of shark sightings, the crew would have a swim. When a shark did show up, we had a study line with a shark hook set in a good-sized piece of meat. We landed a few that way.

"Once, when there were several sharks snooping around, we threw an unattached hunk of meat to see what they would do. The result was absolutely astounding. A real live feeding-frenzy! Seven or eight sharks suddenly appeared, frantically thrashing in a tight circle, biting anything in reach. They were eating each other up. It did not last very long, of course, and I cannot remember if any were able to leave the scene, but it was an awesome sight."

Trumbull said another time "while lying to, someone shouted, 'Hey! Look below us!' Lying just under the boat, as thought basking in the shade, was a giant manta ray, lined up fore and aft with the boat. He lay perfectly still, staying put until we got under way. His wingtips protruded several feet beyond the beam of the boat, and that was naturally all we could see of him. Since the sub's beam was twenty-four feet, he must have been up to thirty feet from wingtip to wingtip. My encyclopedia states that manta rays get up to twenty-two feet wingtip to wingtip, so this guy was a real giant.

"Porpoises are mammals that can detect ships at quite some distances. They come zooming in at high speeds in order to frolic in the bow waves. It's this rapid zooming that can be frightening in wartime. In particular, after dark when the water is phosphorescent, they can be mistaken for torpedoes. But they are fun to watch," said Trumbull. He served aboard the *Cabezon* until 1947.

After *Growler's* fifth run. **William "Stinky" Davis** was transferred to new construction—New London—where he helped commission the SS *Gabilin* on 28 December 1943. Completing four runs in her, Davis was then transferred as chief of boat relief crew in Perth, Australia, and thence to the *Bugara*. At war's end, he went to the Philippines to help set up a sub base there.

At the end of *Growler's* fifth war patrol, Davis was returned to the states to commission the SS-252 *Gablin* on which he made four runs before being assigned chief of the boat relief crew at Perth, Australia.

At war's end, Davis was transferred to the *Bugara* and then to the Philippines to set up a submarine base there. After the war, he was sent to New London to take *Silverside* out of commission and finally discharged from the navy after six years of service at the Great Lakes Station on 26 March 1946.

Photo courtesy of Bob Link

The VFW hall in Littlefield, Texas, November 8, 1985. Rear l. to r.: Hagendorn, Jordan, Don Bergfield (Bill's brother), Link, Davis, Vail. 2nd row, l. to r.: Hilsabeck, Soczek, Sheik, Wade, Lynch, Greenwood. Kneeling, l. to r.: Bialko, Ullrich, Moore, Creeger.

Davis married Elizabeth Sharp, and they have three children—two daughters and a son, and five grandchildren. Davis believes that his Navy experience guided his life and helped him run a successful construction business. His "All Kraft Erectors, Inc." installed machinery and did maintenance work for different companies, mainly Goodyear Tire & Rubber Co. in several states and overseas. He lives in South Fulton, Tennessee, with his wife, and is a life member of the Tennessee Chapter of World War II Sub-Vets.

Rear, Hagendorn, George Wade. Front, Link, Marshall and Holsclaw. Portland, Oregon, 1985.

Leonard D. Greenwood, Southern Regional Director of U.S. Submarine Veterans of World War II. He was elected National President 1994–1995 of the "U.S. Submarine Veterans—World War II," which was founded in 1955 and federally chartered in 1981.

Greenwood's footnote to *Growler's* ramming episode: "One of the badly wounded lookouts was placed in an Australian hospital in Brisbane during February of 1943. When Greenwood last visited him, he brought a carton of Lucky Strike cigarettes and a box of Baby Ruth candy bars—his favorites. In 1978, thirty-five years later, the manager of a local men's clothing store called Greenwood's office to say there was a man looking for him. It was his old shipmate whom he had last seen in 1943 in a Brisbane Hospital. His shipmate had received the Purple Heart and after recovering from his severe wounds returned to the United States to tour the country selling war bonds. The whiskey had flowed like water and his friend became an alcoholic. Years later, Greenwood's shipmate joined Alcoholic Anonymous and became a teetotaler. He told Greenwood of the U.S. Submarine Veterans of World War II. Leonard joined the organization, successfully serving on all levels of the group—chapter, state, regional and national. At the national convention in Milwaukee during 29 August to 2 September, 1996, Leonard Greenwood completed five years on the National Executive Board.

"Years later when the crew of the *Growler* had a reunion in Wade's hometown of Littlefield, Texas, George Wade chuckled when he recalled how he had been carried to the forward torpedo room and saw his good friend, John Baxley who was also badly wounded. George's usual mild manner exploded and he had to be restrained by his shipmates because he wanted to get a machine gun and go to the bridge to finish off his tormentors. That was back in 1984 when Wade and Baxley met for the first time since World War II. The young Lieutenant Commander Schade was there too, also forty years older, but he was now a retired vice admiral. But time slips on by and the memory of pain is forced into a still smaller area of the brain each year and eventually only the good times stand out clearly. Everyone had such a good time in Littlefield that they returned again in 1985, and as it now stands, will again in 1997."

Leaving Growler after her eighth run, **Robert Link** joined Relief Crew Squadron 10 Sub Div 102 in Majuro and Saipan. He then served on the USS *Threadfin* for one patrol at the end of World War II. Link took an honorable discharge on 4 October 1945, and joined the Navy Reserve.

Link married June Shockey and they have four sons: Robert Paul, Mark W., Keith M., and Corey A., and at last count, seven grandchildren. Link retired from the Atlantic City Electric Company after thirty-three years of climbing poles, utility line construction and as a supervisor.

Ed Packwood was on the repair crew after *Growler's* disastrous fourth patrol, when he met his future wife, a Brisbane girl by the name of Ailisa. After serving again on Growler's fifth run, he left Brisbane for New Construction, helping to put USS *Hardhead* into commission on 18 April 1944. *Hardhead* ended its patrol in Fremantle, and Packwood was transferred to repair. Ed and Ailisa were married 30 December 1944. They have two children, Allen and Betty Rae.

Packwood was ordered to Subic where he boarded the USS *Bumper* in July 1945 for his last war patrol. Again, he ended up in Fremantle at war's end, once more on the other side of Australia where his wife Ailisa lived.

Packwood served in the submarine service until late 1952 when his wife lost her eyesight due to a brain tumor. His former skipper on the *Bumper,* Capt. J.W. Williams Jr, now SUBLANT Chief of Staff, arranged for Packwood to serve on SUBLANT's staff, and, as reserve boat instructor until retirement in 1962. Packwood elected Australia as his home of choice.

There he went into refrigeration repair. Sadly, Ailisa's tumor has progressed to a terminal condition.

Louis R. McFall, USN (ret.) served on the *Growler* from the beginning on 20 March 1942 through her tenth run, which ended 30 September 1944. Ten runs, beginning to end.

Five skippers who had known of McFall's outstanding reputation as a radioman and sonar operator on the old S-boats in prewar China Sea Tour, were rolling the dice for him in those early days of 1942. Captain Gilmore, on entering the room, asked what was going on. Their reply was that they were deciding who was to get McFall. Gilmore, as senior officer said if that's the way it was, then, McFall would join the *Growler.*

McFall's vivid memory of her first run was at exactly 10:55 A.M. "As I looked at the clock, the first torpedo hit on that Independence Day in Kiska.

"My tour on the *Growler* was the most outstanding with the three captains: Gilmore, Schade and Ben Oakley. Captain Gilmore and Oakley were lost aboard the *Growler.* The crew had changed completely around me several times. Quite often, I felt quite alone aboard.

Past presidents of the U.S. Submarine Vets of WW II. Bob Link, 1957–59 and Len Greenwood, 1993, with his wife, Jonnie.

I remember several times when we were depth charged. Some of the crew would ask me if I was afraid and I would reply that there was nothing to be afraid of. They always said that 'McFall was the luck of the *Growler*.'

"Most memorable for me was being able to serve under captains H.W. Gilmore, Arnold Schade and T.B. Oakley. This has been very hard to write about. When I do remember, often, I almost cry as Link can attest to, as well as my wife and our friends. I just have to change he subject.

"I have been an loner most of my life, and the loss of the *Growler* has been very hard for me to handle. Thanks for the Good Lord for a wonderful, understanding wife.

"I was one of the last to shake Ben Oakley's hand at the gangway. I have always thought that if I had stayed aboard, all would have turned out okay.

"I left the *Growler* just as it started her last cruise—number eleven."

William Hagendorn, keeper of the *Growler*'s chronicles wrote this tribute in *Kangaroo Express* newsletter about Thomas B. Oakley, Jr.:

"In retrospect, it is now my feeling that Commander Ben, who by his very nature, was a keenly competitive man, brash and unafraid, certainly would have become one of the high scorers of World War II. He made no secret of the fact that he wanted it all or nothing, firmly believing he would win. But, as in many cases, the Jesus-factor was forgotten—Commander Ben got a late start and his bag of luck was too small to start with. Perhaps if so many of the old-timers hadn't been transferred after the last run, that experience that had saved so many times in the past could have done it just one more time. Who knows?"

The *Growler* tragedy is commemorated each year by the surviving crews of the *Growler*. On the 8th of November, 1988, Schade's home Kiwanis Club in Port Charlotte, Florida, had the honor of hosting the commemorative reunion at its meeting place in the American Legion Post 110. In all, two hundred-nineteen men served on the *Growler* in the time that it was commissioned until it was lost. At the time of the Port Charlotte reunion in 1988, there were forty alive and twenty present at that reunion and memorial service. Greenwood conducted the services.

William L. Kuhl was honorably discharged from the Navy 8 January 1946 on Long Island, New York, with more than three years of service. He returned to college and earned a degree in accounting and later worked for Bankers Life in Chicago.

Kuhl met and married Rosemary Pipino in Chicago. They had three children, Cass, LuAnn, and Robert and eventually moved to Ohio. Kuhl passed away in 1972.

There is the story of **Milton Weymouth**, sailor extraordinary. Although there is a partial story about Milton in the U.S. submarine veterans' history book, Hagendorn dug a little and got an almost complete story. It is a salute to their shipmates.

"In October 1961 Milton was invited to be a guest aboard the *Tullibee* on its trial run. At the time Weymouth was a civilian, so why in the world would the navy department invite a civilian aboard one of America's newest fast-attack submarines? The answer was that they were simply showing appreciation for the training that Weymouth had given to junior officers.

William F. "Radar" Hagendorn's personal memorial to his fallen comrades.

Photo courtesy of Bill Hagendorn

"Milt had worked at the 'combustion engineering prototype' of the *Tullibee* after he had completed special training in none other than Admiral Hyman Rickover's program as a civilian, a rare occurrence indeed. They trained both officers and enlisted men of the entire plant, both nuclear and engine room systems. Milt qualified as an engineering officer of the watch as a civilian, then for thirteen years, taught officers and enlisted personnel. In Milt's own words, 'It was like being back in the Navy again.' After leaving there in 1970, Weymouth was assigned to train other civilians on the operation of commercial power plants combustion which were built for the electric utilities. This new assignment permitted Milton to travel extensively throughout the United States including, Florida, Nebraska, Louisiana, Washington, and not too distant from Temecula, to the world renowned San Onofre Nuclear power station in California.

" 'I also got a ride in the USS *Seawolf* as a guest of Hy "Yogi" Kaufman as a result of being head of COMSUBLANT's career appraisal team in March of 1957 which was just before I retired in June of the same year.' "

Milt was born in New Sharon, Maine on 21 November 1919, and enlisted in the Navy just two days after his eighteenth birthday in 1937. His first ship was the USS *Philadelphia,* where he stayed for six months and then was transferred to the old USS *Canopus*, a submarine tender in the

Philippine Islands. He later became a submariner aboard the USS *Pickerel* which was lost in World War II. Milt was returned to the United States (shortly before Japan's sneak attacks on Pearl Harbor and the naval base, Cavite, in the Philippines) on 1 December 1941 so that he could reenlist. After reenlisting he was assigned to the USS *Growler* in Groton, Connecticut. Milton stayed aboard the ill-fated *Growler* for ten consecutive runs, then left just days before the boat sailed out of Fremantle, never to return.

Milt married a beautiful Australian woman named Audrey in December of 1944. They have eighteen grandchildren at last count (1991). A big salute to Milton Weymouth, Jr.

In 1986, **George Wade** was called about mid-August and he indicated he would definitely attend the Baltimore convention, but for the reunion in November—well, he wasn't too sure. While the attendees were in Baltimore the news of George came via a phone call from his wife Jimmie. She said although George's suitcase was packed, ready to go to Baltimore the day before he was to leave, he received word that he was to attend still another *Growler* reunion. This other reunion was to be attended by his old shipmates Gilmore, Kelley, Williams and the other eighty-six crewmen from the *Growler*. George left Monday, August 25, 1986, to attend the largest *Growler* reunion ever, and to the greatest adventure of them all.

Sail in peace, George

Bibliography

Blair, Clay, Jr., *Silent Victory*. New York: Lippencott, 1979.

Beach, Comdr. Edward L. USN (ret.), *Submarine!* New York: Henry Holt, 1946.

Field Enterprises, *World Book Encyclopedia*. 1973.

Fife, Adm. James, Endorsement for Comdr. Howard W. Gilmore, USN, deceased: Recommendation for Medal of Honor—Posthumous.

*Growler War Patrol*s, U.S. Navy

Grun, Bernard, *The Timetables of History*. New York: Simon & Schuster, 1982.

Hagendorn, William F., editor *Kangaroo Express*

Holmes, W.J., *Undersea Victory*. New York: Doubleday, 1966.

Lockwood, Vice-Adm. Charles Andrews, *Down to the Sea in Subs*. New York: W.W. Norton, 1967.

Loomis, Vincent V. & Jeffrey Ethell, *Amelia Earhart: The Final Story*. New York: Random House, 1988.

Rindskopf, Rear Admiral M.H. and Richard Knowles Morris, Ph.D.., *Steel Boats, Iron Men*. Turner Publishing Co., 1994.

Roscoe, Theodore, *United States Submarine Operations in World War II* United States Naval Institute, Annapolis, Maryland: 1949.

Ruhe, Capt. William J. USN (ret.), *War in the Boats—My World War II Submarine Battles*. Brassey's Inc. 1994.

Toland, John, *The Rising Sun*. New York: Random House, 1970.

Wallechinsky, David & Irving Wallace, *The Peoples Almanac #2*. New York: Bantam Books, Inc., 1978.

Wheeler, Keith, *War Under the Pacific*. Alexandria, Va: Time-Life Books, Inc., 1981.

About the Author

Richard J. Lanigan

Richard J. Lanigan's background made him the ideal person to write the epic story of the submarine *Growler*. He has been a close personal friend of the Schades for many years. Lanigan served as a U.S. Army paratrooper in the 82nd Airborne Division from 1947-52 and received an honorable discharge. He has been a member of the American Legion since 1952 and has been an officer in numerous civic organizations and the Charlotte Harbor Yacht Club. A member of Kiwanis, he served as lieutenant governor for the state of Florida.

Lanigan has a B.A. from the Universities of Miami and Florida, and a MBA in international business management from New York University. He has been involved in bank management in Europe and international corporate management on Wall Street. He has been a vice president of a Wall Street firm, a financial consultant and instructor, and president of R J Lanigan Financial Services. He has been active in state and local political campaigns and was founding chairman of the Charlotte County Economic Development Council.

Lanigan has been married for thirty-nine years to Gertraude Schira, a native of Heidelberg, Germany. The couple has two children and twin granddaughters.

The Lanigans live in Laurel, Florida.

Cross section of a

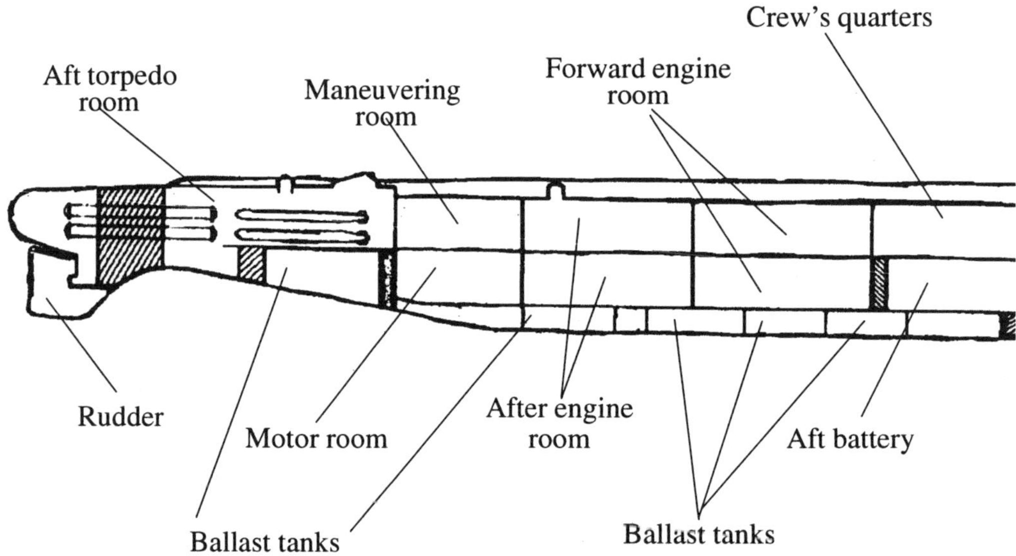